Entering the Divine, One Breath at a Time

An exploration of healing through sobriety and spirituality

Hannah Stinson

Entering the Divine, One Breath at a Time

© 2020 Entering the Divine, One Breath at a Time

Cover Design & Book Design by: David Provolo
Edited by: The Studio Press
Publishing Assistance: The Studio Press

All rights reserved.
No part of this publication may be reproduced, stored in a retrieval system or transmitted in any form or by any means - electronic, mechanical, photocopying or otherwise - without the prior written consent of the author.

ISBN # 978-1-7774397-0-5

*To the women (staff & residents) of Breezy Point
at the Behavioural Health Foundation.
I would not have gotten this far without
the endless love and support from you all.
I am forever grateful for my time spent
with each and every one of you.*

*And to my late Grandma Viv,
who has been with me
throughout this entire journey.*

Contents

Preface. 7

Introduction. 11

Chapter 1:
Cycles of Healing 13

Chapter 2:
When we are grounded, we grow 23

Chapter 3:
Sacred Essence of Your Divine Feminine 31

Chapter 4:
What if wholeness exists within us? 37

Chapter 5:
Release the past in order to add energy
into new beginnings. 45

Chapter 6:
Tune in to your internal power 53

CHAPTER 7:
FORGIVE TO REGENERATE, FORGIVE TO BLOOM. . . 59

CHAPTER 8:
SEEING WITH AN AWAKENED HEART 67

CHAPTER 9:
GOING FROM INACTION TO INSPIRED ACTION. . . 75

CHAPTER 10:
FACE YOUR TRUE NORTH 81

CHAPTER 11:
EMBRACE YOUR SENSITIVITY &
ENHANCE YOUR INTUITION 87

CHAPTER 12:
FEED THE FAITH, NOT THE FEAR 95

CHAPTER 13:
OM NAMO NAYARANI 103

ACKNOWLEDGMENTS 111

ABOUT THE AUTHOR. 115

Preface

I used to wonder if growth was something that was possible for me. I was so used to living underground, ignoring the sweet whispers of my soul, pretending I didn't know that my body was screaming out in agony from the way it was being treated. It was as if the dirt around me had turned to thick, dry mud, and I was being suffocated more and more with each breath. I didn't feel safe in my own body, mind or soul.

Little did I know that the mud would soon soften, and so would my heart. Allowing me to grow as expansive as a beautiful Oak tree; my roots grounded in the earth, allowing me to reconnect with parts of myself I had lost along the way. I began to find myself within the roots of my Oak tree, inhaling these missing pieces as if they had never left. I was growing, becoming more resilient, beginning to understand that I am not a half but a whole. I finally felt comfortable to release the past, so I could live in the present moment with endless gratitude for my future. I reconnected with my internal power and learned to forgive myself and, in turn, others. I started meeting my inner-critic with self-compassion instead of self-hatred. I began to take inspired action, and more importantly, speaking my honest truth. I reconnected with my sensitivity, which allowed me to have faith again. I learned how to surrender, which I have found to be the highest form of alignment.

It was because of my own internal battles that I learned that we need to heal from the inside out. For me, that began with the chakra system and learning how to harmonize and balance from the root up to the crown. If you are unfamiliar with chakras, I will give you my Coles Notes version. The word *chakra* originated from the Sanskrit word, *cakra*, which means wheel. Many cultures, throughout time, have worked with these energy centers. As Margarita Alcantara says in her book, *Chakra Healing*, your chakra system is like your spiritual bloodstream. Our chakras system connects and supports our physical and energetic bodies. There are seven main chakras, along with several minor ones, but for our sake, I am only going to get into the seven main ones. We start at the base of the spine with the first chakra, our root chakra, which represents survival, our core sense of being and family or tribal connection. Moving up to two inches below the navel is the second chakra, the sacral plexus chakra, the center of our creativity and sexuality. Above the navel lies the third chakra, our solar plexus chakra, where our self-esteem and internal power live. The centre of our hearts holds our fourth chakra, the heart chakra, a chakra that represents love and compassion. Next the fifth chakra, our throat chakra, the chakra of communication. The sixth chakra, our third eye chakra, which is located in the area of the pineal gland, is our connection to our intuition.

And lastly, our seventh chakra, the crown chakra, is our connection to our spirituality.

You will notice throughout my book that my roots continue to grow, keeping me grounded. So that I can ascend from the base of the spine upward, allowing my energy to reach *you*. So are you ready to Enter the Divine, One Breath at a Time?

Introduction

Healing, what thought comes to mind when you read that word. Do you think of falling off your bike as a kid and scraping your knee and the time it took for that cut to mend? How the cut went from an open wound to a scab and then was eventually replaced with fresh skin, and you were good as new until you fell off your bike again. Scrapping your other knee and finding yourself back at square one. As children, we don't think of this as being a cycle or pattern of healing. We fall off, we cry, we worry about getting back on that bike, yet, we get back on anyway, and we keep trying, until a few years later we are riding with our eyes closed, yelling "look, no hands!" Recognizing that we have to fall down, scrape our knees and get back on that bike if we want to learn how to ride it is a part of childhood. We learn that even when we hurt ourselves, our bodies know how to heal. With fascination or disgust, we watch our cut go from being an open wound to a scab that we fight not to scratch because we know if we do, it could rip off and go back to that open wound. And if we are able to fight through that urge to itch, we notice fresh, new skin, showing its translucent sparkle as it grows in. Soon enough, our skin heals completely, leaving either no trace of the scrape or a scar that acts as a reminder of the lesson we learned. So whether we have only fallen off our bike once or a hundred times, the point is we get back on. We don't let the knowledge that we may fall off again stop us from trying.

What if we applied this same reasoning to our healing journeys? Remembering that healing comes in cycles, our wounds might be open for years before they start to show any signs of scabbing over. This is just a tangible reminder that healing is happening on the surface. The beauty of our physical bodies is that healing occurs from the inside out. Your skin starts to repair itself from the deepest layer of tissue and works its way outward. So it is only normal when we are in a phase of scabbing over or beginning to see some surface level of healing that we are tempted to itch it, tempted to control the outcome; forgetting that our bodies have the innate ability to heal.

1
Cycles of Healing

The sun rises each day. It doesn't think about it. It just wakes up, stretches its arms, those lovely rays we feel through the crack of our curtain, and shines on our face, filling us with its warmth. With each inhale, the sun rises, radiating its luminescent beauty, spilling over onto every part of the Earth. With each exhale, it releases its energy down into every pore in our body, sinking deep into our souls. Have you ever looked up at the sun while you inhaled? Felt as if you were inhaling the sunshine's rays into your body like liquid light was filling you to the core? That was the moment for me when I truly understood that the lessons I had learned regarding the cycles of healing were true.

If nature has the innate ability to heal and restore itself, and we are nature, we have this natural ability. The sun is living, breathing proof of this, I am living, breathing proof of this; you are living, breathing proof of this. We need to learn to activate this healing from the inside, to see the changes we've made manifest in the outside world. Honouring our own healing journeys, however this activation occurs for you. For me, it was endless amounts of resilience and self-compassion. The more I got knocked down, the faster I sprung back up. I started to view my inner-critic through a lens of self-compassion, recognizing that through all of those years of self-sabotage, it was only trying to keep me safe. Along my journey, there were times when my inner-critic dictated the show; those were the dark nights of winter. I have learned that healing comes in cycles, much like the seasons; winter, spring, summer and fall. These seasons need assistance so that the process isn't so lonely, confusing, daunting and unimaginable. And we lend a helping hand towards these seasons by gathering all we have learned during our spring and summer seasons, so when we do the inner work, no matter the season, we activate a deep knowing within that we can heal.

Just like the seasons, our healing journey will go through cycles. Winter is usually dark, cold and lonely, we can end up suffering from major health concerns if we get stuck in our winter cycle of healing for too long. Spring is the time of new beginnings, if the grass can shoot up through the thick cold dirt, rising again and again, winter after winter, season after season, then so can you. Summer is where we thrive, where we take time to nourish our minds, bodies and souls. The days are longer, allowing us to soak in the rays of sun into the early hours of the night. Fall is when we reap our harvest when we can recognize the healing work we have done throughout our own seasons. But just like nature, we are not always going to be in our spring and summer of healing, where we have profound awakenings and see magical shifts in our realities. Sometimes on our healing journeys, we stay in winter for days, weeks, months or even years. A season where we feel as if we have lost our luster for life and everything seems out of control, or where no matter how hard we try, we keep repeating the same behavioural patterns that don't allow us to move into our spring. Through living with multiple chronic illnesses, overcoming years of past trauma and abuse, as well as through recovering from addiction, I have learned that there will always be those winters. Just like the seasons and cycles of nature, our healing journey will keep following this precious cycle. Allowing us to enhance our connection to Mother Earth by honouring ourselves and letting the inevitable cycles continue.

For as long as I can remember, I've had a strong connection to Mother Earth, feeling her gravitational pulls from a young age. I would be called to dance in the rain or save a drowning butterfly. I spent most of my childhood at my grandparent's home in Willard Lake, about 30 minutes from Kenora, Ontario. This was where I learned and experienced so many firsts, like learning to ride a bike, getting a leech, seeing a UFO (no lie), and where milestone after milestone was met not only by me but also generations before me. Though this was my grandparent's home, it was also our family cottage. They lived there all year long, so I enjoyed the great outdoors no matter the season. From canoeing in the Spring when the ice finally broke, to picking blueberries in the Summer — this was before my allergy, yes I GREW into a blueberry allergy, it is as unfortunate as it sounds — to long trail hikes in the fall, to sledding down the steep and slippery hills in the winter.

I learned to embrace the elements of each season from a young age, literally and figuratively. All of those years, growing up connected to nature, brought me more liberation in my adult years than I could understand at the time. It's helped me see that our healing journeys are much like seasons. As a young child, I felt Mother Earth between my fingers and toes; the grass tickling my nose as I rolled down a hill of dandelions and lush greens. I remember understanding the circle of life as I watched tadpoles become frogs and frogs get eaten by a swarm of tadpoles. But as I grew up, I began to feel this energy of the Earth pulsing through my veins, reminding me that I am nature. If the trees can lose all of their leaves each fall, survive the winter and bloom again in the spring, then flourish in the summer; so can I! Because at our core, our body and souls know how to heal, as Carolyn Myss says, "*The soul always knows what to do to heal itself. The challenge is to silence the mind.*"

How did I begin to silence the mind so I could connect with my soul? I had to take a good look in the mirror and admit that I had a problem with alcohol. I was drinking to numb not only my feelings but my thoughts, conscious and unconscious. I am proud to say, I am a recovering alcohol addict, chronic illness warrior and survivor of past emotional and sexual abuse. My journey to this discovery of self, living in my highest alignment, and becoming an active participant in my healing journey, did not happen overnight. Hell, it didn't happen over weeks or months; it took *years*. Years of self-sabotaging to the point where one day, on January 1, 2019, I woke up and my intuition - which I thought was my grandpa, my guardian angel - screamed, "WTF are you doing?". For some reason, that shook me to my core. Maybe it was because I still had the leftover taste of gin on my tongue from the night before or that I had lost not only one of my favourite pieces of jewelry but also my last shred of dignity. Either way, whatever the reason, I began to walk down this path of recovery consciously. And while doing so, I realized that over the years of learning how to survive in my body, that I was constantly fighting, I gained tools that helped me heal when I didn't know I was healing. The point is, even when we are at our wit's end and self-sabotaging through alcohol, drugs, gambling, shopping, sex, whatever your vice is or was, we are still healing. Sometimes we need to lose ourselves in the dark, cold, Tundra of our winter, for our souls to be woken up to the fact that we are meant for so much more. Our lives don't have to be defined by one season, one chapter, or one experience. After all, it is as wild as the pendulum of life swings that we can truly say, "I have lived." As soon as we can harness this understanding that the wheel of life is forever turning, seasons are always regenerating, and our cells are forever replenishing, we can truly understand that our seasons of healing are inevitable.

I have realized this on my own path and while working with other women who were walking on much darker, scarier and more tumultuous paths than my own. I had the honour of working as an Addictions Counselor at The Behavioural Health Foundation's (BHF) in the women's only program, Breezy Point, for two years. BHF is a non-profit long-term residential treatment center for those recovering from addiction with co-occurring mental health challenges. I began to learn and understand more of the holistic way of life while working at BHF, realizing that this was the lifestyle I had been striving to attain for years with little success because of my alcohol addiction. I was also re-introduced to the 7 Sacred Truths and other Indigenous Peoples' Teachings, such as smudging, drumming, ceremonies and celebrations. One of my favourite teachings, which is one of the most well-known, is that of the circle.

The circle is an imperative shape and part of the Indigenous peoples' everyday lives. This is represented on their traditional lands and within their communities. Their homes were built in a circle, and ceremonies are always conducted in a circle. Some examples are Sweat Lodges, Sacred Circle ceremonies, pipe ceremonies and Sundance. Indigenous people also perform with this element, this shape in mind, with Pow Wows being danced in a circle and the drum representing a circle. When the council is called upon, they form a circle so that everyone is equal, with an equal opportunity to share their truth. What has stuck with me the most is that the Indigenous people see life as a circle. From birth to death, to spiritual rebirth. They understand that humans, just like the seasons, pass through phases, just as the circle of life passes around us. When we fall out of this circle, we fall out of harmony with life, and we block our opportunity for continual growth.

Similarly, when we stay in our winter season of healing for too long, we fall out of the circle of healing because growth can't happen when there is no spring in sight. Have you ever felt as if the only thing to do was to unpack your bags and stay in the cold, arctic winter of your life for the rest of our life? Because I have; I was in my winter season for years before I even became aware of it. But our winters can last a week, a few days or a couple of hours. At the end of the day, it truly doesn't matter how long you were there or how long you have been there. What matters is that you are taking steps out of the bitter, frigid, knee-high snow and consciously choosing to walk towards spring. You are taking steps to find yourself again, blooming and growing along the way.

I started to feel as if missing pieces of my spirituality were flooding back to me, and nature was the messenger. The most memorable feeling of being flooded with my own spirituality was the summer of 2019 when I supported some of our residents and staff participating in Sundance. If you haven't attended, heard of or seen Sundance, allow me to paint the picture. Sundance is a five-day-long celebration where you, exactly like it sounds, dance in the sun for hours as you offer personal and spiritual sacrifices for the benefit of your family or community. The dancers fast for the duration — with the exception of a feast on the last day — in the open air, with whatever weather conditions occur. The dances and songs performed have been passed down through generations, with the use of traditional drums, a sacred fire, praying with a ceremonial pipe, fasting from food and water before participating in the dance, and ceremonial piercing of the skin and a trial of physical endurance. Specific plants and berries are picked and prepared for use during the ceremony, such as sweetgrass, sage and strawberries.

The Sundance ceremony we attended was about an hour and a half outside of Winnipeg, held in a field. I remember driving through the field to park and already feeling the pulsating energy rippling through my body. As my feet touched the ground, I could feel the rumble beneath me, the extreme power of the drumming, dancing and singing, and the power of the earth. As if the stone people, plant people and keepers of the earth were about to break through the thick soil and carry me on these vibrational energetic tides of resilience and strength towards the dancers. As I walked closer, it felt as if my legs had turned to air, as if I was floating on a cloud of wonder. I could barely speak because I was so overwhelmed with raw emotion. I didn't know if I wanted to cry, smile, scream or laugh. It was like every emotion in my body was calling out to be expressed, but all I could send out was gratitude. It's as if I was carrying hundreds of buckets filled to the brim with a gold liquid that represented every emotion possible. The only way to let these buckets spillover was to let gratitude shine out of me like a light that was breaking me open from the center of my heart. As I looked around, taking in my vista of the dancers, the regalia worn, the ceremony itself, the people who were offering support, the sweet and invigorating cultural energy, and the landscape; I started to understand the divine connection we have to Mother Earth on a deep, cellular level. At that moment, I looked up at the blazing sun and thought, "if you can rise again each day, so can I."

This next moment happened when I was six months sober and in a long spring of healing, after years of living and somehow surviving in my emotionless and icy winter. It happened at the perfect time too, spiritual awakenings usually do. I was six months sober and starting to get the six-month itch. I was proud of myself for making it that far but not proud enough to scream it from the rooftops as I am now. To be honest, I was still ashamed because part of me thought, "Can I do this? Can I stay sober?" I was missing the sweet aftertaste of pine that would linger on my lips after I sipped my gin and lime. I missed the warm feeling in my belly and the burning cinnamon in my throat after taking a fireball shot. I missed waking up the next day, trying to find my phone so I could find out what shenanigans went down the night before since I most likely blacked out. I didn't miss drinking or getting black-out drunk; I missed my friends. At first, I became a hermit, knowing that being around my friends while they drank would be too triggering. But as I became more comfortable with the life of a sober girl, I longed for the nights I would never remember with the friends I thought I would never forget. The dynamics changed with some of my friends after I stopped drinking; they stopped inviting me out. Looking back, I don't think it was intentional, but it influenced the intense longing to lose my inhibitions through inebriation. Thinking that if I became Party Girl Han again, then I would get the type of connection that I thought my soul desired.

But when I got to the inevitable six-month itch, I remember thinking, "Six months is long enough, I can handle a shot. Or seven." But as I experienced the intensity of Sundance, the true dedication to oneself through sacrifice to Mother Earth, something that seemed so foreign to me, yet I knew from the tips of my toes to the depth of my soul that it was time for me to do the same. It was time for me to plant my roots and allow the earth to soak up my doubts about my sobriety. So that every time I inhaled, I breathed in the knowing that I was more than capable of continuing on my pebble path to sobriety. It was time for me to allow my branches to grow so high that they kissed the clouds. Bringing all of the compassion, grace and wisdom down through them filled me with particles of energy that fused with every bit of my soul. No matter where I am in my life, my roots are grounded, my branches are supported, and my soul knows it will live on as long as a wise thousand-year-old Oak tree does. Standing tall and proud throughout the seasons, letting the buds on my branches sprout in the spring, like the newfound pockets of sunshine growing in my soul. Allowing myself to flourish in my summer, growing so expansive you can't help but notice. Learning to let go in my fall, allowing the parts that no longer serve me to fall and be soaked up by Mother Earth. No longer surviving in my winter but thriving, because my winter's turned into lessons, lessons allowed my spring to take over organically and the circle to keep moving, healing cycle after cycle. And all thanks to my deep-rooted thousand-year-old Oak tree, allowing me to feel safe and secure within my body as if my root chakra had begun its harmonizing process.

2
WHEN WE ARE GROUNDED, WE GROW

Discovering myself as this Oak tree, with its strong, heavy trunk, its roots that travelled to the depths of the earth's core and its branches that caressed the heavens, was a moment I will never forget. How can you forget the feeling of your feet blending with the soil so that the ground, like vines, wriggles between your toes, slithering up your ankles and calves, as you feel the energy of the earth entering your veins like a morphine drip. While simultaneously, you reach your arms and turn your head to the sky and feel the rays from the sun piercing through your body, almost as if this experience should be painful, but instead, you're breathing in pure ecstasy.

It was once painful, so painful that the only way to handle the pain was to be as numb as possible. Like when you go to the dentist, and you have to get a filling, so they freeze that area of your mouth, and for the next few hours, you are numb to the touch there. You could get whacked in the jaw and feel nothing. Well, imagine that, but instead of it being just in your jaw, it's in your whole body. And not just your physical body, your conscious and subconscious minds. Any time an excruciating thought or bad memory from the past came to mind, I responded with a shot of gin, my preference of poison. Gin, or alcohol in general, doesn't have to be poison for you, but for me, it was like the bottle in the game of clue, with the skull and crossbones on it; waiting for me to take another shot to numb layer after layer of hidden trauma.

    I say hidden trauma because my subconscious mind did an excellent job of covering up wretched experiences from my childhood. Still, memories of these terrible experiences slowly started flooding up through the ocean of gin, no matter how habitually I drank like a fish. I would take shot after shot, hoping I would puke the memories out the next morning and be able to move on, move forward. Instead, my hangovers became my shadow self. I lived for the nights, staying out until 5:00 am and watching the sunrise with raccoon eyes because my mascara was cheap. There was no way after a night of sweaty, booze and drug-filled dancing that I looked remotely close to the word 'good.' I dreaded what followed; the sinking feeling of waking up the next day knowing that all of my demons were waiting for me. It was as if when I opened my eyes, I would look around and see these dark entities all around my room—floating in the corner of the ceiling by my closet, perched on top of the door staring into my soul with their beady black eyes that bled into their even blacker cloud of a body. I made my way to the bathroom, usually crawling, because my body could not physically handle the damage from the night prior and on some level, I thought that if I crawled, the demons couldn't see me. Once I made my way into the bathroom, I would grab the sides of the sink to hoist myself up or slowly attempt to pull myself up, to only make it to the toilet where I would usually sit with my head between my legs, avoiding the sight to come. Oh, and the demons were in my bathroom too, swinging from the curtain rod, laughing at the disgusting sight below. When the time eventually came for me to look into the mirror, I saw the most familiar demon, myself.

It was a vicious cycle. A cycle that lasted years, my winter season of healing lasted eleven years, to be exact. For now, we are focusing on 2017, a prime year for my favourite pastime, self-sabotaging. I broke up with my ex-boyfriend in the spring of that year; it was one of the hardest things I'd ever done. We had a relationship like no other I had experienced at the time, but again, we both had our demons that dominated our subconscious minds, filling our conscious minds with shame, doubt and uncertainty, which seeped into every part of our relationship. Eventually, through some serious binge drinking, molly popping and provocative thoughts, I realized that our relationship was no longer serving me and ultimately no longer serving him. We became like a weird combination of an old married couple and roommates. We barely had an intimate relationship anymore, and we didn't take care of ourselves — emotionally, mentally, physically, you name it, we had all the bad habits, and we thrived off them. The break-up was messy, in every sense of the word. I don't blame him for being as harsh and unforgiving of me as he was. From his eyes, he was blindsided. But from my viewpoint, we weren't picking up on each other's nonverbal cues because we were too infatuated with our agendas. When I finally moved out and put up strict boundaries so that we no longer were in communication, it was like my inner demons had room to breathe fully. So fully that any small shred I had left of my true self was swallowed whole by, dare I say it, drugs, sex and rock-n-roll.

I would wake up smelling of regret, bad decisions, and a lot of egoic confidence that stemmed from probably sleeping with some random "hot Toronto fuck-boy" the night before. And it is with deep regret that I tell you, this type of behaviour started long before I moved to Toronto. The energy of the big city was like permission for my demons to take flight. They would taunt me, ridicule me, some would even applaud me — and those were the worst ones of them all, the demons that feed our egos always are. There was one, let's call her Maybe; this was often my alter ego name when I would go out. If you've watched Arrested Development, you know why. Maybe loved to be the centre of attention, her confidence ate the hearts of emotionally unavailable men, so that this never-ending dance of psychological teasing became so intoxicating as if these men became like shots of tequila. These hangovers of my shadow selves, my demons, started to become an everyday occurrence as if I was living one big hangover. My alter ego made it, so I was intoxicated by the unfulfilling and demoralizing relationships I had with men during the day, and gin made it, so I was intoxicated at night. My shadow self became my only self. I was so deep into the darkness that the only time I saw the light was when I closed my eyes and let the tears pour out.

As Carl Jung said, "How can I be substantial if I do not cast a shadow? I must have a dark side also if I am to be whole." That same year, I visited my dad in Edmonton, and he took me to a cute little bookstore, the Wee Book Inn, where I bought my first book by Carl Jung. At the time, I was planning on doing my Masters and Doctorate in Clinical Psychology. After spending 30 minutes sitting on the floor enveloped in the book, I started to view my demons in a whole new light. That book sucked me in and didn't spit me out until I realized that we truly need to work with the shadow parts of ourselves to see where our light shines through so that we can slowly start to follow the breadcrumbs back to our soul's sweet whispers.

We don't yell at a flower and tell it to grow or try to rush the process and get angry because it isn't happening in the timing that we foresaw for it. We don't dig the Oak tree's seed out because it isn't taking to the soil right away. Just as human embryos contain the plethora of genetic material it takes to grow into adults, plants' seeds do too. In Mother Nature, just as in our lives, everything has its own divine timing. When the seed starts to become a seedling — a baby plant, or Oak tree, for our sake — germination starts to occur. The seed of this hardy and welcoming day, much like a luscious tree, needed optimal air conditions, sunlight, proper temperature, and water for germination to occur. If we were to imagine ourselves as the seed of an Oak tree, we would realize that our environments' conditions have a massive impact on the well-being of our health. Why are we so hard on ourselves? Just like the seed needing the optimum amount of elemental and environmental conditions to be able to grow into an Oak tree that will live to witness the evolution and continue to evolve, we must remind ourselves of the sacred container we are cradled in and have always been cradled in.

This sacred container is none other than Mother Earth. And she is filled with enough space for our seed to grow branches tall enough to touch the heavens above and with roots deep enough to wrap around the earth's core. The Divine Mother has been with us since we took our first breath, and she will be there long after we take our last. I started to hear the Divine Mother's sweet whispers through the steady pulse of a thunderstorm or the grounded wisdom of tree branches and their leaves blowing so effortlessly in the wind. At first, it was subtle, like when you think a fly buzzed by your ear, but you're not entirely sure. But as time went on and I decided to become sober, these calls became so loud that my experience at Sundance solidified more than just the fact that I could conquer my demon, Maybe, and all the other demons that lived alongside or within her. That experience woke my mind's eye up to the ancestral, knowing that I have the innate ability to heal. Just like the root chakra is connected to how safe and secure we feel in our environments, and within ourselves, I could feel myself sinking deeper into my body with an innate knowing that I was healing. Realizing that if I could ground my roots into the soil of my soul in a moment of my life where I felt so unsure and wary of my ability to keep my sober journey going, then they were only going to stay grounded going forward. I was aware of my roots, and I could feel them beginning to sprout out of my toes like the first buds on the trees as soon as spring makes its head. With each step I took, they were rooting deeper into the earth. I could feel each toe grow one branch, then that branch grew its own branch and so forth—each branch representing something that was going to help me along my never-ending healing journey.

The first branch that I felt rooting into the dense, rich soil was resilience. On each breath in, I could feel these tiny branches sprouting one at a time, and on each breath out, each little branch was a memory of a time that I had exuded resilience. Most of these memories come in flashes, much like the blossoming of some flowers, only allowing me to bear witness for a moment before another one bloomed, only for that one to disappear and another to take its place, and so on. As if this one root of resilience, even though it became many, grounded itself to remind me that I have been living with it for longer than my mind can remember, which doesn't matter because it is a feeling that my soul will never forget.

3
Sacred Essence of Your Divine Feminine

If there is anything I know about women, it is that we are resilient. Take a moment to think of your mom, grandma, girlfriend, best gal pal, or yourself. Think of a time when you held their hand through a difficult time. The loss of a loved one, getting diagnosed with an incurable disease, losing their job, whatever the situation, think about how they responded. The response after working through the many setbacks life has thrown at them. Did they get back up? Yes, they did. Did they try again? Of course they did. Because if you looked up the word resilient in the dictionary, beside it would be the word woman. Resilience also gives ode to the ability to recover quickly from difficulties. And as much as we have been conditioned to believe that childbirth is natural and not difficult, it can be one of the most challenging moments of a woman's life and add to her never-ending, abundant river of resilience. As women, or as individuals, we don't need to experience childbirth to know what it's like to be resilient. This is just proof that as women, we are powerful beings who can experience excruciating amounts of pain to bring new life into the world. We are birthed through our mother's womb, and the womb just so happens to be where the sacral plexus chakra is located.

Whether you have a womb or not, you have a sacral plexus chakra, and this is the chakra that is connected to our divine feminine energy, our resilience. To honour the sacred essence of your divine feminine energy is resilience. To allow this resilience to flow in and out of our lives as easy as the breeze floats in and out of your bedroom window, we must learn to cherish this sacred area of our bodies. When we cherish and nurture our divine feminine energy, we start to see sensuality drip into every part of our lives, like the drips of a venti americano, it drips slowly as it fills the areas of your life you didn't know were empty. Honouring your feminine essence allows you to stimulate and activate your sacral plexus chakra, so you can birth your creations into the world, create harmonious relationships, be in touch with pleasure and feel peace and abundance in all areas of your life. When our sacral plexus chakra is out of harmony, it shows up as addictive behaviours, sexual dysfunction, emotional instability, fear of change, and it can even show up as infertility, impotence or menstrual problems. I was the poster child for an out-of-balance sacral plexus chakra.

My sacral plexus chakra was out of balance before I even knew what a chakra, or what menstruation was. I was sexually assaulted at the young age of two by a close male in my life. It is not something my conscious mind seems to want me to remember fully, even to this day after years of different therapy modalities, but I remember feeling absolutely disgusting and completely violated. As a child, I didn't understand that those were the emotions I was feeling; I just knew that what had happened to me was wrong, and my mind did what it could to keep it hidden.

As the years went on, I became hypersensitive to men and their nonverbal cues. I started to pick up on moments where men would sexualize me. In grade three, I noticed the father of one of the girls in a younger grade filming me and some of my other girlfriends during a school performance. I remember thinking it was odd because his daughter wasn't in the performance, and he had the camera pointed at the lower half of my body the whole time. When I was twelve, I remember catching the father of a family friend, gawking underwater at my girlfriends and me in our pool; I made eye contact and gave him the finger, he turned bright red and swam in the opposite direction. I remember thinking, "all men want is sex," so I began to sexualize myself before I even hit puberty. I wore thongs, flashed my non-existent boobs on MSN webcam for older boys at thirteen, and at fifteen, I was hanging out with guys who were not only over eighteen but were also drug dealers. By the time I was sixteen, I had lived in this all too known fantasy of a "good girl" becoming a "bad girl." I was drinking to blackout, drinking to forget my past trauma, drinking to be okay with hooking up with some random guy, and drinking to party. I used to pour half a mickey of Smirnoff raspberry vodka into a cup and add some sprite and be good-to-fucking-go. I began to feel invincible, the rush was contagious, and I wanted more, so I drank more. Throughout the rest of high school, I drank whenever I had the opportunity, which was more often than not.

Before you get this preconceived notion that I was a dropout and druggie, I assure you that I did not fit the category. I thought my true self was a beautiful façade, not realizing that the true façade was my "party girl" self. I was using it as a way to ignore and run from the trauma that I had and was continuing to experience. I started working at fifteen; around the same time, I started down the path of self-sabotage. I started working because I wanted more independence…or more money to get older boys to buy me alcohol, whichever suffices. I was a dancer throughout junior high and high school. I would use my flexibility as a party trick because I knew the guys would over sexualize it, and the validation I yearned for would be spoon-fed to me. I was in the debate club, a part of Youth in Philanthropy, and I was on the Winnipeg Chamber of Commerce Student Council, all of which made me feel like I had a purpose other than the fact that I could chug a Corona faster than a frat boy. I was in touch with my spirituality through witchcraft (yes, I know, a little weird), but hey, I learned that I was a powerful woman at a young age. I was learning to harness my psychic abilities to bring about ripples of change in my life, both wholesome and wicked.

What I thought was my façade of self was my true escape from the toxic reality that I had created for myself. I was in my element when I was honouring these parts of myself, my creative side, my philanthropic side, and my political side. I had a voice, and I was using it! For once, I felt like my best self because I was connecting and embracing these magical aspects of ME. And though I felt like my best self, I also felt incredibly lonely because, at the same time, memories of what happened to me at the age of two started piercing my memory like tattoo needles on virgin skin. It felt painful and foreign, and I didn't have control over when or how it would stop. I continued to drown my pain in alcohol and meaningless relationships with men.

It turned into a pattern of abuse as I attracted relationships into my life with men who had their own inner demons that they weren't ready to battle. Instead of building each other up, we tore each other down, wanting the other to fall off their throne and be sucked up by their shadow self. During one of these relationships, I experienced sexual abuse. I was drugged, raped and left to fend for myself. In another, I was emotionally abused, constantly having to prove my self-worth and being shunned and laughed at when I spoke my truth. I searched for the fragments of my missing self in the broken glass of men with souls who were just as lost as mine. It wasn't until I found sobriety that I understood the damage I had done to this very sacred area of my body and learned how to honour my divine feminine once again.

Sundance was a pivotal moment in my life; the roots of my Oak tree continued to grow from that moment onwards, growing deep down into the earth's core, stabilizing me a little more with each step. As I inhaled, I felt myself breathing in wholeness, which was the second root that grew off my toes, which started to become one with the damp, dark soil. And as I exhaled, I began to recognize that this was a familiar feeling. As if with each breath, I knew that this feeling of wholeness was as innately a part of me as my ability to heal. At the same time, the same feelings of being a powerful preteen "witch" were rushing through me because I was cultivating the same internal energy. The wholeness of the Earth connected in the roots of my Oak tree and were running as deep as the roots of resilience. This time, I finally felt wholeness living not only underneath me, above me, or surrounding me, but within me, and like oxygen, wholeness is always present.

4
WHAT IF WHOLENESS EXISTS WITHIN US?

Discovering that wholeness resided within the stardust of my bones took time and patience, as beautiful things always do. I wish I could tell you that I woke up one day and thought, "wholeness is something that lives deep within my soul, I am whole," and was able to go about my life feeling safe and secure in my own body; spreading this knowledge around like confetti at a birthday party. Alas, riding the waves back to myself was far from smooth sailing. If anything, I capsized more times than I can remember. But because of that inherent resilient nature within, I got back up on that boat every time. And with each gust of wind, the days turned into weeks, and the weeks into months and with each passing moment, I began to question what my cyclic behaviours were so that this cycle I created would finally cease to continue. This cyclical pattern of making myself readily available for unemotionally available men needed to stop, and this was because I was finally starting to question the idea that I was somehow half of a full whole. As if my sacral plexus chakra had woken up to the fact that it was out of whack and was ready to be healed.

Growing up, I remember hearing from family, friends, society, and the media that, as humans, we are looking for our other half. I was conditioned to believe that I needed someone else to complete me, to make me feel whole. No wonder why so many of us search for love, companionship, or in my case, validation in other people! It's like the pursuit of meaningless sex and codependent relationships, both of which seem like a double rainbow, gleaming with opportunity and potential. You follow the rainbows to what you are certain is going to be a pot of overflowing gold (love, abundance, security, whatever your gold is), only to find a troll sitting there, smiling his snarly, 'I told you so' smile. Because when you get to the end of that rainbow, it is always the same feeling of disappointment. And never with the troll, always with yourself, because there is something, like a fly buzzing by your ear, telling you that this search for your 'other half' is bullshit and that you are as whole as you need to be, in this moment and all the ones to follow.

Before I finally breathed in my long lost connection with my divine femininity, I had to hit rock bottom of my own promiscuity. I lacked self-worth, I didn't respect myself, especially not my body, and I started to believe that I deserved this life I created for myself. It was as if I thought it was an honour to be me, to be living a lie as a closet alcoholic and chronic illness sufferer. Part of my lack of self-worth stemmed from my diagnosis of endometriosis. The textbook definition of endometriosis is "the presence and growth of functioning endometrial tissue in places other than the uterus that often results in severe pain and infertility." My definition is "a debilitating chronic condition that causes chronic fatigue, brain fog, periods that cause you to black-out from the pain, pain when ovulating that is often worse than period pain, pain when having sex, chronic nausea, chronic diarrhea, and the constant struggle to stand up for yourself and what you're experiencing because of the constant gas-lighting by the medical community, your peers, and past partners." Was that a run-on sentence? Probably. But the point remains, this condition can take over your life, and my way to cope with that was drinking, drinking to the point of blacking out. I was suffocating in alcohol to the point where I couldn't remember if the night before was painful or not.

At the same time, I was struggling to be taken seriously by my doctors and other health professionals, which took a significant toll on my emotional and mental health. I started to lose the desire to want to speak up for myself or ask for help. I had been screaming from the inside out to be sincerely heard for almost a decade, and every time I asked for help, it was never granted or received. I was either ignored, forgotten about or told that "the lactose in your birth control pill is what's causing your pain," "you're overreacting, it's just a bad period," or "you can't seriously be complaining about your period pain again?!" I slowly began to become a recluse, to shutdown. And just how the reptilian brain of a butterfly knows when it is the right time to hatch from its cocoon, my habitual instincts kicked in, and my reptilian brain told me to shut down and try to heal myself in the only way I knew how — my old friend self-sabotage.

As we know, this was my winter of my healing cycle, a winter that lasted eleven years, with some spring's here and there, maybe an hour of feeling like my true self, allowing me just a moment to bask in my summer, reap my very tiny harvest in the fall, only to be back in my winter a few hours later, drowning in gin. I searched for the missing pieces of my feminine energy, trying to fill a void that felt so large that every time I took a breath, it was as if I was being sucked into the black hole of my soul. I was suffocating in darkness, it was like looking up at the night sky on the night of a new moon and feeling the darkness envelop you with each inhale, but instead of being nourished by this presence of new beginnings, I felt lost, as if I lacked the potential to live the life of my dreams.

Alcohol had a grip on my soul, I lost connection to all the parts of me that reminded me I was whole. I scattered my sacred femininity over the hearts of men who were far more deserving of love than the love I ever gave them. I didn't love myself, and I didn't care to learn how to love myself. Loving myself looked like doing six jager bomb shots in a row and then twerking on top of a bar. I remember one time, in first-year University at Ryerson, I was dancing on a stripper pole that just so happened to be on a bar top, screaming at some guy who called me a slut, "I am a fucking feminist!" and then proceeding to make out with three men I had never met before. As much as I felt like a "fucking feminist," I wasn't being liberated by making out with three men as it was coming from entrapment of my own traumas. Can you see the pattern? As much as I thought that I was liberating my soul by letting my freak flag fly, I was just adding bars to the cage where my soul was being held captive. These weren't your regular metal cage bars, no, no, they were shards of sharp glass, with each shard shooting up another, a chrysalis that seemed never-ending. Every degrading memory was stabbing my soul, it was like groundhog day, so I drank it away.

My journey to sobriety started on January 1, 2019, I woke up knowing that this life, ***my life***, of being so irresponsibly naïve, needed to ***end***. I was soul-sick, I yearned for more than the mundane, repetitive cycle I had created for myself of getting drunk or dying trying. At the end of February 2019, I was diagnosed with liver disease and much to my surprise, it was not from my alcohol abuse. My liver was 75% covered in tumours because of long-term estrogen exposure, aka birth control. I had been on birth control for eleven years and hadn't had a period in seven years as a treatment for my endometriosis since my periods often had me debilitated for weeks at a time. I had always inquired about the risks with long-term estrogen exposure at the extremely high dose that I was on. Alas, doctors reassured me that there was a very low risk of anything happening. It turns out my condition is one in a million or something jaw-dropping like that. But hey, I am a miracle baby, so what else do we expect here? Not only was I two months premature, it was a miracle that I was born as my mom had severe endometriosis. It has been an overwhelming experience, but from that moment on, at the end of February

ENTERING THE DIVINE, ONE BREATH AT A TIME

2019, I reminded myself that I am the creator of my destiny, that I can call back the missing pieces of my soul through the sweet song of sobriety. And with a twinkle in my eye, I looked to the sky and felt the wind brush against my skin, it felt like a kiss from the heavens, granting me the motivation needed to persevere. The missing pieces of my soul began flooding back through nature, and my creative juices started to flow again! The stagnant energy of inspiration was no longer stuck, it was being fed by the pink, purple, orange and blue prairie sunsets that stop you in your tracks; by the nostalgic feeling of sand between your toes; and by my feminine essence shining out through my creations. It was as if my sacral plexus chakra was feeling the love as I birthed these creations through me, organically and without attachment. So the messages could rise up like kundalini energy, as the ascension of my soul was occurring, and it was magical. These messages from my soul started as whispers, as they always do, but the more time I allowed myself to do the things that made my heart sing, the louder the voice became.

My heart began to sing in tune with my sweet song of sobriety. The more I showed up to my yoga mat, the more time I allowed myself to paint without purpose, the more meditating, breath-work, prayer and card reading I did. It became so melodic that my soul was able to ride along the invisible musical bars with grace and ease so that these messages were the lyrics, and my heart sang them back to me. The message that stuck out the most came to me like a lightning bolt shining so bright in the dark thundery sky, it's as if the clouds separated to send a message.

One side of the cloud is the notion that I am some sort of half who needs another half to make me whole. And the other side of the cloud representing the truth, my truth, that I am already whole. Wholeness not only exists within me, but it also thrives off the fact that I have acknowledged its presence and that I am more supported on my healing journey now than I ever have been before.

I became aware of the wholeness within me by recognizing that my own wholeness would not have occurred if I had not accepted my past as lessons learned. I believe that our pasts do not define us, but that doesn't mean that they don't influence our present lives. Therefore, when my next Oak tree root began to plunge deep into the damp soil, it represented the lessons I have learned throughout my life, the lessons that allowed me to flourish and grow. Because if it weren't for this octopus-like tree root, my beautiful, brimming branches wouldn't have grown into the flowers that have supported me along this journey. We are both light and darkness, I wouldn't be where I am today if it weren't for my lessons learned. The difference between now and then is that now, releasing the past is as organic as exhaling.

5

RELEASE THE PAST IN ORDER TO ADD ENERGY INTO NEW BEGINNINGS

It is important to remember that every decision that we have made in our lives was the best decision at that time. We made it with the most evidence possible, within our reality, at that moment in time. If we made mistakes, well, we LEARNED, and when we learn, we GROW. As the saying goes, we grow through what we go through.

That is why it is imperative that even when you are in your dreaded winter season of healing, you are still taking steps towards your spring. Even if your winter is a season that is so cold that you can see each breath in a cloudy fog as you exhale, know that there are blades of grass waiting to rise through the thick soil, just as the missing pieces of your soul are trying to grip their way back into your consciousness. You are still growing even when your seed feels stuck under the earth with no escape route. And I say this because I have lived it. I survived in the winter season of healing for over a decade. Feeling separated from my soul and fighting my own body but all the while still blossoming internally.

When a flower blooms, it doesn't think about who is watching it or who is around to see it in its full, shining glory. It blooms in its divine timing, staying open and not dimming its light according to who walks by. The flower doesn't strive to seek validation from its surroundings because it knows that its natural essence is powerful enough. This natural essence is like a perfume that we all wear, unique to our soul; I guess you could call it soul perfume. The scent of your soul perfume gets stronger and stronger as you trudge through the mountains of snow, helping it to melt to reveal vines between your toes and the smell of spring under your nose. An organic reminder that you have been blooming all along. Even if each step took years to take, you still travelled forward, even if it was in a sideways manner.

And if there is anything I can tell you about the path to healing — or any life path— it is *not* linear. If anything, the path reminds me of the board game, snakes and ladders. Just as in life, when you are climbing up a ladder, maybe a ladder you've been climbing for years, and you're inches from the top, about to hoist yourself up and over to the other side when a snake comes along and takes you down a few notches. Whether it was a small garter snake, like an unexpected parking ticket that might set you back on your car payments, or a boa constrictor that rapidly and randomly burns your house down, these snakes shake us to our core and cause us to either fight, flight or freeze. When the amygdala is working on overdrive — which can happen when we have been living in our winter season for too long, naturally getting us, cyclical beings, stuck — we tend to let any and every obstacle be a boa constrictor.

I used to believe that my life experiences were happening *to* me, with no rational thought in my mind, that maybe they were happening *for* me. That maybe every experience, traumatic or not, was a lesson to be learned—a chance for me to see the person behind the curtain. But of course, during my seemingly unbearable winter years, I couldn't even notice that there was a curtain to pull back. There was a lesson to be learnt, but I wasn't ready. I needed to fall into my drunken snow angel state of being a little longer before I could recognize that the snow around me was melting, and I was just rolling around in the dirt.

My diagnosis of endometriosis and how I was treated by men in previous relationships in regards to this condition did a number on my mental and emotional health. I started to devalue my womanhood because I assumed that people would either pity me or not believe I could be a good friend, partner or employee, because of my endometriosis. Instead of wearing it like a badge of honour like I do now, I kept that badge under lock and key; only allowing it to be worn when I was in debilitating pain or having a flare-up that was so severe that everything else in my life had no choice but to be put on hold. I was afraid to be honest because I had lost friends in high school who didn't understand why I had to cancel plans last minute or missed almost a week of school every month because of my period. I was fired from jobs because

I wasn't honest about my condition, which affected my ability to work, but I didn't want to be labelled as disabled or just plain unable, which in my mind somehow seemed worse. Relationships had ended time after time because I didn't want to be seen as vulnerable. I did not realize that my vulnerability would become my superpower. I was placing judgement on myself, creating my snakes and allowing them to take me down as I willingly let go of the ladder.

    I had to release my past by birthing my creations, using art to express my pain, something that's as second nature to me as putting on your seatbelt when you get into a car. I had to be honest with myself about the nature of my health, so I could, in turn, be honest with others. I had to be open to receive the love that we're all warranted, to be reminded that I was more deserving of love at that moment than any other before. I had to release the old, selfish, judgmental, closed off Hannah, who thought she was not capable of being the woman society wanted her to be because of her endometriosis and past emotional, mental and sexual abuse. Like somehow those were my fault, as if I said, "pick me, pick me, give me a chronic health condition that has no cure and the lack of self-worth that comes from being abused," and asked to endure an internal battle of constantly giving away my power to external forces. Releasing that old version of me didn't happen all at once, and I am thankful that I didn't need to add spiritual psychosis to my list of health conditions. It was like the onion of my soul was being peeled back, layer by layer, so that my soul perfume could drift up and replace the pungent onion with saccharine smells of lavender and honey. Each time a layer was unwrapped or fell off, my soul perfume became a little fiercer. This fierceness began to show up in a slowly evolving, newly forgiving and unapologetic me.

Naturally, my fierceness showed up first through my art. In the last three years, I have showcased my heart and soul through two different art exhibitions. In March of 2017, *Love Thy Lady Parts* made its debut in Toronto, Canada, as my Capstone project for my Undergraduate Thesis from Ryerson University's School of Fashion. As endometriosis is a condition that I live with, I saw my capstone as an opportunity to bring awareness to the condition and educate about endometriosis. Endometriosis is a condition that affects women's reproductive organs as an extraordinarily debilitating and invisible disorder, with no cure and limited successful treatment. My main objectives of this exhibit were to successfully communicate my and other women's experiences with endometriosis through art and technology, with the hope to enlighten the public in understanding this condition. I wanted to showcase that endometriosis, a monthly cycle of suffering, can be translated creatively through art and can be a positive form of relief. My exhibit showcased my artwork, photography, and designs to successfully communicate the experience of living with endometriosis, both through my own experiences and the experiences of the women I interviewed. This exhibit included interactive art pieces, paintings, photography pieces and sculptures, to name a few. And in December of 2019, *Feminae: Hidden & Revealed* was held in Winnipeg, Manitoba, as an ode to my journey thus far, as well as an ode to women and the female form. There were over 50 pieces of my art, which represented my own female identity. The pieces exhibited were how I viewed myself and the lens I wanted the rest of the world to view me through. The one lens that I wanted to change was the way people view vulnerability. Because vulnerability is often considered a weakness, but vulnerability is a strength. I was raw, honest and vulnerable about my experiences living with multiple chronic illnesses. So I asked the audience, "can you be a little more vulnerable with yourself? I did, and it helped cultivate Feminae: Hidden & Revealed."

Even though these exhibits were held years apart, both of them allowed me to peel back more layers than I ever imagined possible. These experiences allowed me to come to terms with areas of my life that I thought were as closed off as my ability to access the psyche's true depths. I subconsciously released doubts and uncertainties about myself through my art. My paintbrush was the liberation of my self-imposed ideals about my lack of abilities to be a wildly wealthy woman. With each brushstroke, I became further aware of my gleaming potential. I put my life on the line through my art, letting the world bask in my vulnerability, while I soaked up the fact that this feeling of vulnerability was making me more fearless on each inhale. So on each exhale, I did precisely that, I feared less. My exhibits were tangible results of attending to and nurturing my sacral plexus chakra, so I could be cracked open to release past energy that I held in this sacred area of my body.

Allowing myself to stay cracked open and vulnerable was the most challenging part of releasing the old me. It was the layer that I so desperately wanted to hold onto, even though it was barely hanging on by a thread. Understanding that I could be truly loved again happened when I least expected it, as meeting a fairytale prince always does. In my winter season of healing, I was still parachuting MDMA and doing body shots of tequila off my girlfriends, living in Toronto, working on King Street by day and well, partying on King Street by night. Now I don't want to sound cliché, but I did meet a prince one night, back in September of 2017, a beautiful adonis of a man, who was infatuated with me from the moment we met but I was too preoccupied with getting high to realize. After some drinks and swift moves on the dancefloor, I started to see the twinkle in the prince's eye, learning this twinkle was for me. He was an actor, so he had to drive eight-plus hours up to northern Ontario to film the next day. We stayed in contact over text, as one does nowadays. As we got to know each other more, we started to realize these synchronicities that made me feel as if we had known each other for lifetimes. He treated me with respect; he gave me butterflies, not just in my stomach but from my head to my toes. He was like my prince charming, only wanting the glass slipper to fit my foot. Even though we only spent a few nights together, it was as if he was the reminder that I needed to know that I deserved this type of fairytale love. From that moment on, I released the idea that I wasn't worthy of the knee-buckling, palms sweating, heart burning type of love, because I was. The prince showed me that. Even though the relationship was short-lived, the lesson I learned about love changed me for the better.

I finally understood that releasing my past was adding energy into new beginnings. It was allowing me to see all of these past experiences as beautiful lessons. So that with each step I took, my legs, my Oak tree roots, began to penetrate deeper into the earth. Allowing my next root, of internal power, to grow so hefty and cavernous into the soil that the smell of my soul perfume enveloped my Oak tree, allowing the aromas of lavender and honey to satisfy and nurture my inner flame.

6
TUNE IN TO YOUR INTERNAL POWER

The ever-burning eternal flame, much like the solar plexus chakra, craves nurturing, caring and tender-loving devotion. If we neglect this truth, we run the risk of the flame burning out. Whether it burns out for a few hours, days, or in my case, years, it can come alive again. It is not impossible to nurse the flame back to health. Much like the whispers of our soul, our internal flame isn't always accessible, especially if it has burned out or never been given a chance to burn brightly. When we don't tend to the burning logs on an open campfire, we allow the sparks to die down and the fire to extinguish. The new firewood — the potentials of our future — are no longer being tossed onto the crackling kindling, so it is no wonder it would burn out. When we lose hope for our brightly lit futures, our inner flame can burn out, leaving only a wispy ring of grey smoke that seems to carry our dreams away as fast as they appeared. Leaving the residue of the soft, fragile ashes sprawled across the ground, like smears of your soul, left to be blown away, just as easily as your dreams, which have now seemed to have gone up in smoke.

My eternal flame had been put out time and time again, whether from a torrential downpour from a hot, summer storm; or a prevailing gust of wind that it stood no chance against. I had allowed my flame to run dry because I didn't see the necessity of nurturing or tending to it. I had become accustomed to giving my power away, allowing it to be nourished by external forces. Not having a clue that my inner flame was still intact, waiting to be remembered so that it could burn so high that with each exhale, the flames would shoot out of my mouth, reclaiming the power that I had willingly or unwillingly given away. Because calling back my power was the perfect kindling for relighting my flame, this flame, like a fire pit in my belly, fuelled me to keep going, to believe in myself and my dreams. It wasn't until I got sober that I had realized I was surviving off of external influence, feeling incredibly drained, and at the time, blaming it on my illnesses, stress from my work, or other external forces. First and foremost, I gave my power away to alcohol. It was my safe space, my coping mechanism for so long that I was blinded to the fact that my inner flame had become a pile of ashes. But my soul was waiting to rise from the ashes, ready to burn again, and that is exactly what happened.

Before I go any further, I want to discuss the differences between external and internal power, also known as the external and internal locus of control. External power is influenced by outside stimuli. When we are running off external forces, we turn to alcohol, drugs, relationships, the media, shopping, peers, and the list goes on, to stimulate us. This type of consumption is fatal for our inner flame. Instead of allowing the sweet smells of our soul perfume to ignite the flame and listening to our intuitions, we turn to those who we think have the answers for us. Internal power is when we allow our soul to guide us; instead of turning to someone or something else. The beauty of enhancing our connection with our solar plexus chakra is we can go within and communicate with our inner flame, allowing it to burn higher and higher until living from a place of internal power is all that we know.

In our society, we are taught to be consumers. It is our learned behaviour from a young age, it's almost inevitable that we would give our power away unintentionally day after day, year after year. And I am not sharing this to make you feel guilty or bad if you have been living from a place of external power, I am sharing to help open your beautiful eyes to the fact that you can be living from your internal source of power, your inner flame. Living from your internal power enhances your self-worth, allowing you to be more in touch with your inner warrior, cultivating states of peace and calm, and finding a balance between your material and spiritual worlds. If I can do it, so can you, because there is no magic potion out there waiting for you to guzzle it whole, the magic potion is your internal power. And if I could begin to sing along with the melody of sobriety, I knew that calling back my power would be the spark to light and keep my soul on fire for this lifetime and all lifetimes to come.

So how did I begin to call back my internal power and become

ENTERING THE DIVINE, ONE BREATH AT A TIME

the badass powerhouse I am? I became an active participant in my healing journey. Remembering that I am a whole person, and to own my inner authority, I would have to do the personal development needed to feel ready and safe to call back those missing parts of me. Taking my health into my own hands was the driving force behind my want to ride the waves of my life instead of allowing them to drown me. But before I learned how to surf the tsunamis, I had to be tossed around, like when you're swimming in a lake or ocean, and you get caught under a big wave. You're twirling in circles, feet overhead, not knowing up from down or when or if you'll see the surface again. That is how it felt before I took my healing into my own hands and began to call back my internal power from the lost lands of my psyche, on this energy plane and beyond. It was as if when I made this decision, the waves that had kept my lungs full of water, refusing to let me breathe in my potential, finally subsided. The storm didn't calm itself; it was me, I was able to calm myself. It was as if my body floated effortlessly to the top of the water, just as effortlessly as those lost pieces of my soul started flooding back, acting as the kindling for my eternal flame.

Becoming an active participant in my own healing journey opened my third eye to the importance of honouring myself and where I am at that moment. I had downplayed my chronic illnesses for years, refusing to come to terms with the fact that I was sick. And that I will always be sick to some extent. But that doesn't mean that it is *all* of who I am. Endometriosis, liver disease, and even the trauma that I still carry in my trauma backpack are just small parts of me. They don't make up my entire being, and when I finally became aware of that, it felt less daunting to invest in my health — emotional, mental, spiritual, physical, physiological, psychological, all of it — because ultimately, I was investing in myself.

This allowed me to be honest about my conditions with myself and the people in my life. It was a big step for me when I was asked during a job interview in 2018, "what is the biggest obstacle you have overcome?" and I responded with, "living with endometriosis and still showing up and giving my passionate energy to everything and everyone, every day, even though I am in excruciating pain," and guess what? I got that job on the spot. And even though I didn't stay at that job for more than two years, I remember leaving that day and feeling the sunshine radiate through my body, as if it recognized that my internal flame had just been lit a little more and elevated a little higher. That experience allowed me to continue to be open and honest about my truth so that when I met my boyfriend, the love of my life, my best friend and confidant, my soulmate from this life and all lives past, I let my past trauma, experience living with chronic illnesses and more spill out of me like verbal diarrhea. And over a year and a half later, through a long-distance relationship, me choosing to get sober, me being diagnosed with liver disease, Covid-19 putting a halt on my moving plans, we are still together and stronger than ever. Being open and honest with him at the beginning allowed a level of communication — along with being long-distance — that I have never experienced in any other relationship.

ENTERING THE DIVINE, ONE BREATH AT A TIME

I remember thinking that the prince showed me what fairy tale love was but looking back, I realized that he was just another frog, and now, I am with my prince, and together we will grow to become each other's king and queen.

Finally, allowing my soul to be seen for its incredible multi-faceted nature was rejuvenating. It was as if every pore in my body finally took one big, deep exhale and released all of the external power that I had ever invested in. With each breath in, I was able to absorb all of the benefits of living from a place of internal power. I could feel the roots of my Oak tree being impregnated with bountiful acceptance of myself. When the next root started to intertwine with the others and grow deeper into the earth, I recognized it as fast as you would your first love in a sea of strangers. This new root from my Oak tree was one that I had avoided tending to for longer than I could remember. My root of forgiveness felt small and powerless. But I knew with my eternally burning flame, forgiveness was about to become as organic to me as putting one foot in front of the other because, at the end of the day, forgiveness is a stepping stone to healing.

7
FORGIVE TO REGENERATE, FORGIVE TO BLOOM

"The greatest native warriors weren't the ones who wounded the most people; they were those remarkable beings who had such personal power that enemies lay down their weapons rather than fight." — Denise Linn

The ability to lay our weapons down instead of keeping on fighting is the epitome of forgiveness. Whether we deny forgiveness to ourselves or others, fighting to hold on to something that is meant to fall away or refusing to let go of something that is no longer serving us, the result is the same, we are only hindering our rebirthing process. When we forgive, it allows old energy to be released so that new energy can dance its way in and help to begin the regeneration process. That way, our soul perfume can allow the eternal flame to keep burning and the flowers in our wombs to start to open, instead of withering away.

If forgiveness seems too daunting, like a small task on your to-do list that keeps being pushed until tomorrow or the next day, the next week, the next month, until before we know it, that little task that seemed like no big deal, a year later, still isn't complete. Now it isn't so small. It has become a lot larger, and it weighs on you. That task could be applying to go back to school, resigning from the job that drains you, or making that doctor's appointment to get that weird pain in your stomach checked out. Whatever the task is, the fact of the matter is you are still in the same place as you were a year ago, which is nowhere. And nowhere on the path to healing is incredibly daunting. It's like being in the void, where nothing and everything exists at once. Where you feel like you're drowning and floating at the same time, suspended in air, but your lungs are full of water. This same void can ooze into the mind, body and soul when you refuse to forgive. We can't expect ourselves to move on from people, situations, experiences, limiting beliefs or past trauma if we haven't forgiven ourselves first. When we judge, criticize, or express hate towards ourselves, we block the regeneration process and aren't able to move into our spring cycle of healing. We create a barrier around us, like the thick wall of ginormous, sharp thorns that shield the forest in Sleeping Beauty, where Maleficent lives. These thorns stab away any potential growth energy before it even has a chance to make its way to you.

When we are showing up day after day with the same old behaviours and beliefs, sometimes we fail to reflect on these patterns. As breath-taking as patterns can be, if you stare at them for too long, your vision becomes fuzzy and the pattern quickly becomes overwhelming. According to Dictionary.com, a pattern by definition is "an arrangement or sequence regularly found in comparable objects"; "a regular and intelligible form or sequence discernible in certain actions or situations." Both of these can be related to how we allow old conditioning to take over and be our source of power, just like we can or have allowed our locus of control to be determined by an external power.

In regards to a pattern being an arrangement of comparable objects, we can compare this to how a lack of forgiveness causes us to let past situations influence present-day ones. For example, let's travel back in time to my first relationship with my ex-boyfriend in high school, who probably to this day wouldn't consider us having been "in a relationship" since *gas-lighting* was his middle name. Speaking my truth has always been something that, like math, hasn't come easy to me. I often find myself getting choked up before I can get the words out, as if my tears are trying to protect me from speaking my truth. In relationships, speaking my truth was as foreign to me as running a marathon. In my very first relationship, when I was only fifteen, I was shut down when I tried to express my truth. This led to being ridiculed and, later on, being sexually abused. After two toxic years of dating on and off, I had allowed my voice to be silenced to the point where, for the longest time, I blamed myself for that night. My ex-partner didn't give me the space to feel safe to speak my truth; that bled into my other relationships like a rushing river. The kind that if you get pulled in by the current, you're unwillingly being thrashed around by waves, knocking into rocks and having trouble seeing up from down, left from right. Every relationship after I allowed my voice to stay silent for fear of being shut down once again. I unconsciously stopped the regeneration process of healing by not forgiving myself for past tendencies of keeping my voice at a mere whisper when it came to how I felt. It was easier to beat myself up for it instead of forgiving myself for the fact that I wasn't in supportive environments during those times.

It wasn't until the fall of 2018 when I finally woke up to the fact that I was allowing this passive behaviour to become a pattern of comparison, and I knew that I had to actively break the chain. I had ended up in a relationship with a real gem, cue eye rolls from every one of my girlfriends, he really had me convinced that the way things were going, were good. Deep down, I knew that things were anything but, because my intuition would yell at me to "get out." It was that Fall after an intense sound bowl healing session at my yoga studio that I woke up to the fact that it was time to let the tears flow until they ran dry, leaving nothing but my words of genuineness to be sung from the heart. Forgiving my younger self for not standing up for herself with the power of her words. Reminding her that she is safe now, that adult Hannah is holding her, that she can begin to release the past notion that she won't be heard. Doing so opened up the floodgates to breaking the pattern of comparison and its detrimental effect on my ability to forgive and ultimately to heal. When I forgave myself for my lack of communication in relationships, it was like adding one hundred logs to my internal flame, there was no letting it burn out now because my voice became the kindling.

And that kindling allowed my internal locus of control a

chance to flourish in its own fire. But first, I had to understand that in order to truly forgive myself and others in my life, I had to break the pattern of actions that had become customary because of my past coping mechanisms of shutting down and not speaking up. When we repeat these unhealthy patterns, we are continually hurting ourselves and others. When I began navigating through the Western medical system after my endometriosis diagnosis, I was met by constant medical gas lighting, so I began to believe that no doctor would believe me. Believe that I was in pain, believe that I was suffering as much as I was, believe that my quality of life was being stripped from me more and more, each time aunt flo came to town. Even though I was diagnosed with endometriosis in 2016 after having laparoscopic surgery and ablation of the endometrial tissue, I was still met with an attitude that I was overreacting or somehow embellishing the truth of my chronic pain, fatigue, brain fog, nausea, diarrhea, the list goes on.

Shutting down in this area of my life was not only hard on my mental health, as we know, but it also contributed to my past of self-sabotaging. And yes, this self-sabotage was me drinking like a fish, drowning in gin and soaking up every ounce of toxicity, but it was also me not believing in my ability to heal or even ask for help anymore because 'no one believed me.' I began to block my ability to receive the help that was necessary for my healing cycle to continue in order for me to make it through my winter and into my spring once again. After my exhibit, *Love Thy Lady Parts*, I realized that my voice mattered and that I didn't have to sit back and be a passenger on my healing journey, I could step into the driver's seat and take full control. Because I had to write an undergraduate thesis paper to accompany my exhibit (Capstone Project), I began to learn and understand more about endometriosis than most, if not all, of my doctors. When it came time for appointments, I was going in with a list of questions, answers that I had come up with for my treatment plans but also being open and willing to take in the suggestions from the professionals that I was sitting in front of.

This was when I began to bloom as if with each inhalation, the flower in my womb began to open, and with each exhalation, the petals grew thicker and silkier, allowing this full bloom to be the receiving door. Allowing me to receive the help that I deserved and was warranted because I wouldn't take 'I don't know' for an answer. When I moved back to Winnipeg from Toronto at the end of 2017, I decided that was when I needed to take my health into my own hands because at the end of the day it was no one's responsibility but my own. Today, I have many people and healing modalities that help me maintain not only my physical health but also my emotional, mental, and spiritual health. I practice yoga, meditation and pranayama (breath-work) daily. I use art as a form of creative self-regulation. I am a spiritual self-care advocate, using my Oracle and Tarot Cards daily, praying, practicing energy healing and qi flow. I work with an Art Therapist, a Focusing Practitioner, an EMDR Therapist, an Energy Healer, a Massage Therapist, a Pelvic Floor Physiotherapist, an Indian Head Massage Therapist, Floral Essence Practitioner, a Reiki Practitioner, and I have five coaches (a business coach, a mindset coach, a money mindset coach, a marketing coach and a book coach). I now follow a very strict diet. It has taken me three years to get to a place where I feel as if I can eat and not get sick (most days). I don't drink alcohol or caffeine. I don't eat soy, corn, dairy or red meat, this is known as the "endo diet." I follow the FODMAP diet, eating foods with low FODMAPs as they are easier to digest. I also recently started following an Ayurveda-inspired diet, which is based around yin and yang energy, also known as sex and stress hormones and how you can use foods and spices to help balance. Along with all of this, I am constantly reading and educating myself. Three books have changed the way I view being an active participant in my own healing journey - *When the Body Says No, The Hidden Cost of Stress* by Gabor Mate, *Balance Your Hormones, Balance Your Life* by Claudia Welch and *The Anatomy of the Spirit* by Caroline Myss.

The moment I forgave myself for being chronically ill and all that has come along with it, my eternal flame no longer needed igniting, the flame was lit, and my solar plexus chakra was in equilibrium. My flame was ready to burn eternally and burn away any unwillingness to forgive myself and, ultimately, others. I was finally on the right trajectory, my Oak tree was growing taller every day. With each inhale and exhale, the next root began to plummet its way into the earth, not allowing me to think twice about the magic it held. The next root was so encompassing that I couldn't help but feel its transcendent energy as it was the root of self-compassion. Growing so wide and so expansive that the energy it held was so powerful. It felt as if it was shooting up from the souls of my feet, all the way to the crown of my head. Knowing that this vast vigour of self-compassion was ultimately love. With each step, this adoration energy became as sweet and invigorating as my soul perfume; and I began to hum one of my favourite Beatles songs, *All You Need is Love*.

8
Seeing with an Awakened Heart

I used to be disgusted with the idea of love, my heart chakra was closed off to the world. The love I had been exposed to growing up wasn't necessarily unhealthy, but I developed an unrealistic relationship with the idea of being loved. Not in love, I couldn't care less about opening the peony within my heart to share my secrets and dreams with someone. No, I just wanted to be loved. I sought out validation from men, and as we know by now, I let those relationships control me like a puppeteer. These men as Geppetto, directing the courses of my strings, but even worse, me as Pinocchio, allowing myself to be controlled. And every time the submissive power took hold of me, the petals on the peony in my heart began to wilt, shrivel and fall away. Just as the blood of my womb drips down and out of me, the petals do the same. Leaking through my veins and travelling down to exit through a canal of creativity and life energy, only to leave traces of mourning. An emptiness was left behind in my heart, that caused an unquenchable thirst for unconditional love. But to get to a place where unconditional love was all I knew, I had to rip the truth Band-Aid off. My truth was that I was running from opening up my heart and my soul. I was living in true avoidance. Never allowing my body to merge with my soul; so that my soul could open up to me first, and not my body to some Geppetto.

From a young age, I began to understand that love is hard, and it hurts. My parents have been divorced for most of my life, though we did live as a family for a couple of years, that memory is but a glimpse on my timeline. When I was in elementary school, I was one of a few children of divorced parents — and I already felt isolated being a highly sensitive, shy kid — but this only amplified the feeling of loneliness. I didn't understand why all of the other kids' parents lived together and why I lived with only my mom, and I only saw my dad a few times a year as he lived in Ottawa. Of course, my inability to understand why my parents had to make the decisions they did, turned into this feeling of longing. A longing to be loved. But as the earth made its way around the sun many more times, I began to disassociate from this feeling of wanting to be loved in fear of seeming needy. This fear energy became a magnet to distressing situations with men, allowing myself to fit the mold of what the man I was with wanted. Instead of revealing my soul perfume, I let it wash out of me, just like the petals of the peony fell out of my womb. My lack of boundaries only enhanced these experiences as I let my heart be ripped out of my chest again and again. I would pick up the broken pieces and shove them back together, forcing them through the cavity of my chest, tearing open my ribcage in hopes that my heart would go back in. But it fought, it tried to refuse, it bled, it attempted to wither away as the peonies did, knowing that it wasn't being nourished in the body that it was in. My body rejected my own heart because it refused to allow love to be a vying factor in its life force energy. My heart was rejecting me because I was rejecting love, and love represents the heart's vitality. It's why it pumps blood throughout the body. But for me, there was no blood to be pumped. It was like my body became the void, allowing nothing to exist but caused everything in me to wish for existence.

One evening in 2017, when I was trying to force my heart back into my chest, I realized that there wasn't anywhere for it to go because of the void. The void would suck it whole, and even though I had scorned the idea of true love for so long, I knew I wasn't ready to lose my one chance to gain back the verve of my soul. What my body needed was boundaries, and from that moment forward, the healthy boundaries around my mind, body and soul began to flourish like vines up a lattice, covering every empty space that craved for unconditional love.

Becoming aware of my boundaries, or lack thereof, became more evident to me, the longer I continued down my journey of sobriety and ultimately of healing. In my second year at Ryerson, one of my electives was the Psychology of Design, and we did an activity where certain class members volunteered to participate, myself being one of them. You could say that it was my "go-getter" attitude, or maybe I was buzzed from my gin and juice in my thermos, I will let you decide. Either way, I gathered to the front of the classroom, along with 15 to 20 other students. The professor asked us to make two lines and stand across from one another. She told us that she was going to tell each line to walk towards the person they were standing across from, the one standing still would say "stop" when the person walking got too close to their personal bubble. When it came to my turn to stand still, the guy walking across from literally came right up to my face before I said, "stop." I remember my professor looking at me with a worried look in her eye — literally, no one else had anyone stop nearly as close as I had — I just laughed it off, and we all went back to our seats. She then went on to explain how spatial awareness is imperative when it comes to design — in particular, interior design and working with a variety of types of individuals. I did this exercise six years later when I was sober and working at the Addictions Treatment center during staff training on Non-Violent Crisis Intervention. My personal bubble had increased in size, and in that moment, I became aware of just how unconsciously I was giving my energy and power away in my past. I had to excuse myself to use the washroom only to catch my breath and ground myself in the present moment. As I sat on the toilet, in a tiny washroom that was located underneath the stairs, I felt the walls caving in towards me. My memories began to drip down the sides of the walls, like tar, heavy, dark and glutinous, ready to asphyxiate my mind, taking me to the past, like the tiny washroom was a time machine. I was transported effortlessly throughout the times in my life, where I willingly and unwillingly allowed my soul to be confined by the people-pleasing archetype that I had created for myself. I soon came back into my physical body, and the tar turned back to the fifty-year-old peeling beige paint, it occurred to me that it was time to heal this archetype and let the part of me who refused to put the needs of my soul first return to its natural state of being, love.

Allowing myself the grace and permission to become aware of my lack of boundaries and heal the people pleasing archetype I had created for myself, even long after I stopped drinking, had to be done with self-compassion. Otherwise, my self-critic would take over and dictate my every move. To understand my self-critic and its very needed role, I had to meet it with as much self-compassion as I could. Think about when you're tending to someone you love who is going through a hard time, you wouldn't tell them to hurry up and get over it, to move on, to be stronger, more challenging, more resilient. No, you would console them, remind them that they are loved and supported, that they will get through whatever it is they're stressed out about or struggling with. Just like you would wrap that loved one up in a cozy blanket, see your self-compassion as the cozy blanket for your inner-critic. Allow yourself to meet your inner-critic from a place of love and understanding. Remind yourself that its job has just been to protect you. Even if it hasn't been protecting you in a sufficient way. The thing about our inner-critic is, it doesn't stop doing its job. It wants to keep you safe, and your self-compassion is there to remind it that you are safe. So the next time you say "no" when you mean it, your inner-critic might want to shut you down and make you feel bad for putting yourself first. But remember your self-compassion is wrapped around it, allowing its warm and amorous energy to permeate into your inner-critic, reminding it that putting yourself first is an act of love. This is how we build the protective energy needed around our personal bubbles, by honouring what we want in our hearts, and sometimes that is just saying "no."

Practicing saying "no" was a game-changer for me. I could feel the blood beginning to pump through my veins again, and the void disappeared like the pop of a blown bubble. Learning that my inner-critic was just trying to help protect me and hold me all of these years stung my heart. I felt the pang in my hand, looking down and taking a deep breath as I held my heart in my hands; my whole heart, and not a bunch of shattered fragments. On my next deep inhale, I could feel the cavity of my chest opening slowly and softly. As I exhaled, my hands, holding my heart, floated towards the center of my chest, allowing me to place it back where it belonged, in me. My body was like the cozy blanket of self-compassion, keeping my heart safe so that I could take the necessary steps towards loving myself unconditionally so I could love others the same. I could feel my heart chakra begin to sing in tune with the sweet melodies of my sobriety.

Learning to love myself unconditionally meant accepting every aspect of me, even the dark parts that I had been running from for what seemed like an eternity. Deep down, the roots of my people-pleasing, lack of self-worth, hating my body because of my chronic illnesses were dead and ready to be ripped from the soil of my heart so that new seeds of opportunity, growth and transformation could shine through. I decided instead of ripping these roots out with malice, shame and remorse, I would pull them out with compassion, gratitude and adoration. Because of all of those harsh derootings, I let whoever walk all over me, whether it was in a personal or professional setting, were lessons in self-love. These lessons allowed the pieces of my heart to fuse their way back together so that I could see each and every experience forward as a lesson, as Caroline Myss would say, actively engaging my symbolic sight.

Instead of allowing the lessons to live off me, living from these lessons was a catalyst on my healing journey. Learning that my heart and soul were one once again, not only existing in harmony but thriving in harmony, was a breath of fresh air. Glorious, nourishing air that I had tasted long ago and was again drinking. So when I took my next breath in, my next root, the one of inspiration, started to penetrate its way into the earth below me. I could feel the light liveliness it held. As if the root grew larger with each inhale and exhale, and the nimble pieces of the shining bright light danced like fairies through my body and into my heart, so that my child-like spirit could fuel this inspirational root that was now a part of me. So it could grow up through my body, into my branches and to the heavenly skies above.

9
Going from Inaction to Inspired Action

Inspiration, similar to kundalini energy rising from the base of your spine, can come from anywhere and at any time. Your rush of inspiration can come from floating in an open body of water, seeing a flower growing in concrete, hearing the crack of thunder and watching the lightning dance across the sky during a summer storm, the setting sun, the rising sun, the waning moon or seeing the balsamic moon. However, and whenever it arises, don't try and stop it. It will only cause inaction. When we block the creative flow, we end up burning out the internal fire we have worked so hard to keep lit. The inspiration that sets our inner flames ablaze becomes a form of a storm in and of itself. The torrential downpour that floods our minds with dreams of the future. Winds that cut like glass, spitefully whisking away your hopes for what could come next. The Hindu Goddess Kali channelling her empowered energy into the thunder and lightning, hoping to wake you up and out of this state of staying still. Only you wake up in the morning to see the wreckage, searching for the pieces of your soul in the mud of what now holds the branches of trees that once caressed the sky, only to realize the pieces of your soul have been washed away along with your dreams and hope for the life you have always longed for.

This, my fellow divine beings, is because of our sneaky old friend, inaction. Inaction likes to show up just like our inner-critic does, with the intent to keep us safe but in reality, it is just causing more harm than good. Inaction is that little voice that says, "you can do it tomorrow," "it's too hard, I better not try," "I am not good at *insert literally anything here* so I can't do XYZ," "I don't have the time right now," "I can't afford to." I am sure by now you are familiar with your voice of inaction. You can probably think back to a time or many, where you let it take the driver's seat. It is not an easy thing to view inaction from a place of self-compassion, but when we do, we begin to understand why it's working so hard to hold us and keep us safe. Inaction wants us to be comfortable; it wants us to stay where we are. Because staying where we are, in an environment where we're familiar with the atmosphere and the results of living in that particular energy brews the same energy. When we feel that jolt of inspiration, we must act on it, even if all that means is focusing on consistent daily action to get us to our goals. Consistent daily action will always bring you to your goals. And consistent daily action comes from inspired action. So why do we tend to lean towards inaction? In a world of instant gratification, it is almost impossible not to be accustomed to getting what we "want" when we want it. The beauty of inspiration is that it requires a follow-through. Our dreams don't manifest by us just wishing them true. They manifest with consistent daily action and by the fire of inspiration that is lit in our souls, ready to keep us safe and warm, in a much brighter and supportive way than inaction ever could.

My voice of inaction was procrastination and indecisiveness, both of which kept my throat chakra closed off, keeping my voice hidden because it seemed like the safe thing to do. I have always been a dreamer, an old soul with a child-like spirit, wanting to explore, indulge, and feel every bit of what the incredible thing called life has to offer. All too often, my voice of inaction drowns out any potential for inspiration to shine through. I have been an artist since I was knee-high to a grasshopper. Expressing myself on a canvas was the first form of creative self-regulation that I experienced. This then spilled over into other aspects of my life - dance, theatre, creative writing, cooking, sculpting, the list goes on. But for some reason, I never went farther than the first step. It was in my winter seasons of healing, the years of alcoholism and after, that I felt the energy of inaction takeover. That glass of wine or gin and water was much more important than working on finishing my advanced illustration project or updating my resume. Even as I embraced sobriety, the procrastination of finishing any task that had the potential to better my future often seemed too daunting. I would wait until the last minute and thrive under the pressure I put on myself, getting done what needed to be done and reaping the benefits. The more I began to understand that my voice of inaction stemmed from wanting to keep me safe because it was worried I would fail, the more times I was able to wrap it in the warm cozy blanket it needed. As self-compassion is the warm blanket for our inner-critic, it is the same with inaction. I would wrap it up tight like a tasty, sizzling, veggie burrito, knowing that I can't eat burritos, so all the more reason to focus on the inspiration that was feeding my soul. Once you love yourself unconditionally, your inspiration rises up from your soul and not your ego.

There were many times throughout my cycles of healing that inspiration took the driver's seat. It was almost as if my inspired self, my soul-self, said, "move the fuck over ego, I need to shine for a moment here." Now, these moments are everyday occurrences, as I am always taking inspired action. But long before I arrived at this present moment, I had to learn from these snippets along my timeline and hope that my soul was fed a little more each time. So that one day, like today, it would be living in my whole body, and not just in my fingers and toes, but also in my ears, eyes and nose. In the past, my inspiration would leave as quickly as it arrived. Like a monarch butterfly fluttering around you on a sunny day, it flounces around you only for a few seconds then it's gone, and you're left wondering where its magical self has gone off to. Just like that thought of what would enhance your business, help you move into the house of your dreams, help with your exercise routine, your skin regime, your spiritual practice, your finances, your, your, your…what was I going to do again? And all of a sudden, you're back where you started, which was inevitably nowhere. Taking inspired action meant jumping in head first, even if the water was murky and deep, my consistent desire to keep swimming was the consistent daily action that allowed me to manifest my dreams.

It all started with my yoga practice. Through years of dedication, hard work, learning and unlearning, I was able to push myself beyond any and all perceived limitations I had about my physical body. Being chronically ill, I often thought that I was "too sick" to build muscle, strength and endurance. That was just my inner-critic, once again, trying to keep me safe. The voice of inaction, not wanting me to try a headstand in case I fell and hurt myself. Instead of listening to that voice, I wrapped it in a warm blanket and took the time needed to build the strength to properly invert. My longtime goal in asana — the physical practice of yoga — was to be able to do the pose, Scorpion Pincha, which is an inversion where you balance on your forearms, while your legs and feet curl over your head, creating almost a "C" shape with your body, in theory, physically representing a scorpion. In July of 2020, I accomplished this incredible posture after years of consistent, daily action. And that didn't mean inverting every day for a year and a half. It meant, shoulder strengthening, core work, spatial awareness, as well as understanding anatomy and how to properly invert to not injure myself.

I have never been a patient person, I used to get anxious about the ever wavering unknown, but yoga taught me how to bring patience off my mat. I became a much calmer, more grounded and heart-centered human because I adopted the "patience is a virtue" outlook. And this understanding changed the way I viewed myself and my ability to act upon the intensity of my inspired action. It is allowing me to breathe the power of inspiration into everything I set my mind to. Taking my dreams and goals for the future and breaking them down into small, achievable tasks. So that now, as I complete my Yoga Teacher Training and enter into my Yoga Therapy training, I am not only living in my own manifested dreams, I am working towards achieving the certifications. Because it is incredibly easy to, at any point, give up. The work is hard, it is time-consuming, it is but another thing on my never-ending list of "to-dos." But the beautiful thing about all of my "to-dos", is that they are pieces of my soul. My business *Healing with Hannah*, my personal life, my alone time, all stems from my soul self. The positive influence of inspiration has become so riveting it's as if I am being spoon-fed this never-ending stimulus.

Allowing my child-like spirit to shine through, ensuring that the idleness of my inaction voice was content, as the effervescent clouds that embodied my inspiration floated around me. And it was as if these clouds of inspiration activated the next root within me; starting as an inch in my left pinky toe, I felt a twitch as the new root of honesty began to sprout so effortlessly out of me, the Oak tree. My throat chakra finally felt nurtured so that it was safe to shine, safe to speak my truth no matter how much my voice shaked. Allowing me to stand even taller and prouder, finally facing my true north.

10
Face Your True North

Standing tall, facing my truth north was not something that came easily to me. I have put blood, sweat and tears into calling back my power through the power of speech. For me the power of speech started with creating art, then dance, and then creative writing. It flowed into modeling, yoga, photography, poetry, singing and drumming, chanting, life coaching, card reading, energy healing, and inherently, writing this book. With the knowledge and awareness of my lack of boundaries and having them be rebuilt into a gangrenous root in my Oak tree that is filled with my inner wisdom of always putting my own needs first, I was able to begin to speak my truth. My throat chakra began to harmonize so that speaking my truth allowed me to be honest with myself. At this point on my healing journey, I took a step back, relishing in these roots of my soul, feeling their nourishment rushing through every part of my body. I had grown so vast, so expansive, in such a short period of time, it was powerful to bear witness to but my legs, like the trunk of my Oak tree were drained. They needed the root of honesty which was now becoming as enormous as the others. I spent so much time catering to the physical needs of my body and accepting the truth of my past instead of continuing to keep it frozen in the winter of my healing. This allowed my soul to sprout new buds every spring, and these buds were recognizing that I was keeping myself hidden, because I was used to staying small. Finding reasons to stay quiet, instead of speaking up and growing tall.

Facing the truth that I had become passive with my voice, allowing it to be snatched up by people, experiences and situations, like Ursula holding Ariel's voice hostage in The Little Mermaid. It was a hard pill to swallow, a pill I choked on many times, gagging before it finally went down and stayed down. This pill opened my eyes to realization that, like Ariel, I would do whatever it took to be liked, to be included, wanted, appreciated, validated, and so on. Ariel gave up her voice to be with the man of her dreams, foolishly believing that a malevolent creature like Ursula would play nice. Much like me staying silent, naively following suit of others on my path, I allowed my voice to be shut down, ridiculed, and forgotten. But when that pill finally absorbed into my gut, I inhaled a sweet message from soul perfume reminding me that I am a goddess and I chose to treat myself as one. From that moment on, **I chose to be beautiful**, radiating my unique essence from the inside out. Allowing my radiant qualities to shift the vibration of the planet. I started to nurture my unique essence, I cared for it, supported it, and I began to naturally ascend into the best version of myself.

For so long my soul essence, that was intrinsically my voice, had been neglected, shut down, demoralized so often that my energetic and soul self shrunk. I struggled to find my voice after selling it to many Ursula archetypes. I searched for the lost parts of my soul in other people, experiences and situations, easily forgetting that what I was really searching for was actually lying quiescent in me. Waiting to be nurtured, longing to be heard. So that I could stand tall, continuing to embrace this journey I was on while refusing to stay silent, facing my true north. Speaking my truth meant being honest with myself about my passive behaviours in the past, recognizing that at the time I made the best decisions I could with the information that I had, whether it had been internal or external.

I was also reflecting on the past moments along my own timeline where I had activated this part of me. When I was in my adolescence, working through the emotions of puberty, as well as the parts of me that had been violated, I felt like I was trying to escape from quicksand. I would try so hard to express how I felt but the words wouldn't come out, instead uncontrollable sobs were released. Which resulted in me sinking deeper into the quicksand. But when I started journaling around the age of eleven, I started writing letters to the people who I struggled to have conversations with, like my mom; and this became a healthy habit of release. Whether I ended up giving the letter to the person it was addressed to or not, I was able to exercise my own strength, honouring my anger by giving it a channel to express itself.

These channels were support systems along my healing journey.

Dance was my savior during the peak struggles of my high school days. I danced for over a decade and during high school, I was dancing four to five days a week. When I danced I felt free, I let my stress, pain, worries and fears seep out of me through endless pirouettes, chenes, and jetes. Expressing my passion for something I loved so intensely because it gave me a voice. When I worked as an Addictions Counsellor, I had the marvellous opportunity to be a part of their singing and drumming group, the Soaring Eagle Singers. They met five times a week to practice and I joined whenever I worked. I remember the first time I participated, I had tears in my eyes the whole time. I could barely sing because I was feeling such raw emotion. I focused on the thump of the drums, doing my best to stay on beat, as I also did my best not to let the tears roll down my cheeks. The first song I learned was the Strong Woman song and I swear I felt the divine feminine energy that resides within us and all around us, strike me through the chest as it cracked open my heart. The message of the lyrics sent shivers down my spine and my heart began to feel something I never felt before. An activation of righteousness occurred and from that moment on it would be impossible for me to stay taciturn. I recall walking back from the Traditional site we had on the large property, to the house I worked at, feeling the power of the earth. It was as if Mother Earth was foreshadowing what was to come in the near future when I attended the Sundance ceremony. This reflection was like a breath of fresh forest air, encouraging me to explore new channels of communication to express myself and exercise my freedom of speech.

I began to live as the Goddess Saraswati without fully becoming aware of it until writing this book. Saraswati is the goddess of self-knowledge and is considered to be the personification of knowledge. When prayed to or invoked through mantra, chanting or other forms of connecting with the divine, she ensures that the artist finishes the painting, the writer finishes the book and the student passes the exam. As Meggan Watterson mentions in her Divine Feminine Oracle Guidebook, Saraswati encourages us to look within to the deep knowledge we all possess because the essence of who we are, will flow effortlessly into everything we create. It was becoming honest with myself by utilizing my self-awareness that I saw that I had the tools to continue to grow and heal. That it was safe to speak my mind, stand up for what I believe in and not take anything personally since I am not responsible for how someone responds or reacts. I am only responsible for myself and that included speaking my truth. Because being honest with myself, allowed me to in turn be honest with others and it was a powerful transformation.

Which is how it felt when I started honouring my voice, facing my true north and speaking my truth. It was as if it all began to flow effortlessly like a rushing river of clear blue waters, so clear you could see the glistening pebbles underneath. This river helped me heal with each word I spoke, while I sang every note, it liberated me to not give up, to keep swimming. Because I knew that the speaking of my truth would create a domino effect so prominent, it would influence those in my life to do the same in their own divine timing. This rushing river runs deep within us all. Just like a new wave crashes against a dense rock in its wake, my next root grew so fast that within the blink of an eye, my root of sensitivity appeared beneath me. But it grew differently than the others, instead of shooting down, it grew in a sideways manner. Intertwining with all of my other roots, growing through them, protecting them, energizing them. I could feel that this root of sensitivity was going to be a sacred container that I was longing to be held in.

11

EMBRACE YOUR SENSITIVITY & ENHANCE YOUR INTUITION

Embracing my sensitivity was the key to unlocking the door that acted as a rite of passage into my intuition or reconnecting with my third eye chakra. And on the other side of that door was, as Clarissa Pinkola Estes would say, "the river beneath the river." The rushing river of my intuition was just waiting for me to cannonball in, making waves along the way. Because trusting the rush of my intuition, riding the waves that I would create along the way, meant making a big splash and rocking a few boats in the process, if necessary. My intuition didn't care if I failed or looked like a fool. It cared that by listening to its sweet whispers, I might actually cause people to think in a new way. Because like every great trailblazer before me, I was ready to make some waves and ride the river beneath the river that lies within the depths of my intuitive soul.

I learned from a young age that my intuition was whispering sweet truths to me every day. And I learned to listen to these truths that tasted like sweet skittles on my tongue from my parents, always telling me to "listen to my gut." This allowed me to tap into my intuition subconsciously at a very young age, knowing when to trust a stranger or not, feeling as if I knew how to proceed with a situation that most my age would need assistance from adults with, all on my own. As I began to grow into the woman I am today; these sweet calls were watered down through my own limiting beliefs, doubts, fears and worries, to name a few. They were flooding the cries from my soul, drowning them whole so that the river beneath the river began to dry up, instead of breathing in new life.

In every moment I can remember along the timeline of my life, I have always been highly sensitive. As a kid this showed up in being "too emotional", always crying often even in moments when most people wouldn't even shed a tear. Now it shows up in messages from the divine through the kiss of a butterfly, warming me up from the inside out, knowing that it was my late grandma who gave me that kiss. Or the soaring of an eagle overhead, showing up right after I said a prayer to the heavens, tears filling my eyes knowing that my message is being carried to the Creator above. Reminding me that if I stop to pause and listen, my intuition will remind me it is continuously pouring itself into every aspect of my life, in tangible and intangible ways. But when I reflect on those moments where I could barely put a sentence together, I remember being able to sense other people's emotions without them speaking. Growing older I absorbed emotions, energies and feelings that weren't mine but had no idea that was the case. I went from being my usual bubbly, loving self, to feeling overwhelmed for no good reason. But as time passed and I grew into adolescence, I was continuously bullied for being "overly emotional" so that by the end of Junior High School, I thought that in order to be liked, I had to "not give a fuck". Which of course was not in my true nature, I was a lover, not a fighter. But that was the attitude I adopted and little by little, the voice of my intuition went from being crystal clear to barely a whisper to nothing at all.

For almost a decade, I barely communicated or listened to my intuition, it was almost as if when someone would mention that "we have all the answers we need within us", I would have to stop myself from laughing out loud. I had fooled myself to the point where I couldn't begin to fathom that you didn't need to seek outside sources or validation for what you were feeling. It was a foreign concept to me that most often if we sit silently enough, we can begin to take note and hear the calls of the melodies that come from the waves of the rivers of our intuitions crashing along the shore lines of our souls. My addiction to alcohol was a true inhibitor of my ability to connect with my intuition, to embrace my sensitivity, to feel truly connected to my third eye chakra. It was as if the alcohol was the poison to the river, causing it to turn to sludge, just like the blood that was attempting to pump through my veins. The toxicity I was experiencing was happening throughout every aspect of myself, especially my energetic self. It was as if my aura turned black, inviting in energies of angst, destruction and volatility. It was like I was living in my very own groundhog day movie; experiencing the same situations over and over again, refusing to come to terms with the fact that I was actively repeating these behavioural patterns, manifesting these situations over and over again. This was the Universe's way of trying to teach me a lesson. It never lost hope that I would finally learn the lesson. Playing out these karmic relationships until I understood that the so-called bad karma I kept experiencing was because I had lost touch with my intuition. These karmic relationships showed up romantically and platonically; as we know I would consistently attract emotionally unavailable men but I would also attract females into my life who were just as emotionally unavailable. Time and time again I would be left heart-broken, down on my knees crying out for a second chance, even when I knew that a second chance was going to be another drop of poison into my river. When I wasn't granted that second chance, I would pick up the pieces of my broken heart, shove them into my pockets since at the time they no longer belonged in my chest, moving onto the next insalubrious relationship that would inevitably leave me right where I started, broken hearted and deaf to the cries that were screaming to be heard.

It wasn't until after my very messy break-up in 2017 that I slowly started to embrace my sensitivity and find my way back to being BFF's with my intuition once again. As if the mountains of snow from being in my winter cycle of healing for so long began to melt because that was the incentive needed to bring me into the next season, the next cycle, spring. And as the snow melted, the frozen river of my intuition did too and the ice began to break away, to reveal the rushing river underneath. My intuition, still alive and intact, still flowing with creativity, ideas, life force energy! To access this innovative energy, I had to begin to embrace my sensitive side again, something I had neglected doing for so many years that it was almost like beginning again. And how fitting was it that I felt all of this occurring at the pivotal moment of spring, the time of rebirth, of starting new, of tending to the new seeds in the garden of my body, mind and soul.

Learning to embrace this warm emotion, allowed me to melt a little more into my own soul. Breathing into this intertwining of my emotional and spiritual selves, felt like I was communicating sweet whispers of truth to myself once again, a feeling I remembered as if it was yesterday. And these sweet whispers were shared to me by my intuition, my very first soul sister. It took me over a decade to admit that my intuition had guided me through everything I had experienced in my life so far, and that I had made my decisions by either listening to it; or as we know not listening to it because I wasn't privy to the messages at the time. Because I was able to remember that my sensitivity was and is the sacred gateway to my intuition, I learned that like anything else, to strengthen it, I had to actively practice embracing it. And eventually these whispers become as crystal clear as hearing someone say your name from a few inches away.

When I first started to actively exercise the muscle of my intuition, when I began to wade into the waters of the river beneath the river, it meant sitting with sad, painful and uncomfortable emotions. Emotions that I had run away from for so long or drowned out with gin because it was easier than sitting there, feeling them creeping in around me like shadow people. But in reality these emotions that felt like shadow people were only making their way closer to me to hold me, to hug me, to bring me into their embrace and remind me that feeling is a part of the process. And that sitting with them was going to be the only way out because the only way out is always through. Moving through means I wasn't going to be unpacking my bags and living with these uncomfortable yet extremely necessary emotions. It meant that I was going to be a never-ending passenger on this current that had me flowing down the river of my intuition. Over the last couple of years, as I've learned to embrace the rapids, the waves, the pelts of water that have continuously splashed at my face, I started to love the fact that I will never again be out of touch with my river beneath the river. That even when I need to swim to shore, leave the riverbank, take the soft pebbled path back to the physical plane that is my reality, the river is still there, guiding me every time I close my eyes and connect within. And when I closed my two eyes, my third eye could open and I could see the magic being woven right in front of me.

The more I began to connect with my intuition the more magic and synchronicities I began to attract. The magic I experienced was because I answered the calls instead of just witnessing them to be. I switched careers from Communications and Design to working in the Holistic and Mental Health field with little to no background because it was a call from my intuition to do so. I paid off all of my debt and started my business with but a couple hundred dollars to my name because my intuition reminded me that I was in a safe place to do so. It held me in the sacred container I had been dreaming of, allowing me to make every decision when it came to my personal and professional lives based off of my "gut test" and trusting that the physical sensations I felt were tangible forms of communication from my intuition. I started receiving messages from within during breath-work sessions, card readings, meditations, prayer and yoga. These messages included but were sure as hell were not limited to, when to launch programs and promotions, the creation of content and coaching programs, the amount of clients to call in; as well as, when was the safest time to have medical procedures, when to make my move to be with the love of my life in Edmonton. All of which had their own incredible snowball effects, one of which being writing this book.

Embracing my sensitivity on a continual basis has been the gatekeeper to connecting with my intuition on such an intimate level and harmonizing my third eye chakra. Allowing me to surrender to the sweetness of my life and float along the river beneath the river even when I don't know where it is taking me. Learning to trust the twists and turns of the river bend, guided me to notice that the next root was beginning to descend from and out of my body. This next root would've only been able to develop after all the others were cradled by the root of sensitivity. Because in order for this root, the root of faith to grow, I needed to first reconnect with all of the roots along the way. So I could begin to truly feed the faith I had and have for my wildest dreams to come true instead of the fear that my dreams are just that, dreams.

12
FEED THE FAITH, NOT THE FEAR

When someone says "have faith," what comes to mind? Do you picture something biblical, a pastor in a church reminding you that God is guiding you, and all you have to do is ask for that guiding light to show you the way? Or does a memory pop up? Of a time when you were told to have faith in a relationship that was sucking the life out of you. To have faith that you will get the promotion, when in fact, you really wanted to quit your job. And maybe none of these resonate with you, maybe having faith in all that is holy is something that has come naturally to you as if you don't know anything else. But for me, this was my reality. My crown chakra longed to be tended to but I didn't and at the time couldn't understand that having faith that all will prevail for the better meant that, the better will come. All I knew at the time was living from a place of fear.

I started feeding the fear at a young age. Well I should say, the fear was fed to me at a young age. When I was in grade one, there was a little boy who threatened to kill me. I can still see his face when I close my eyes, and it sends shivers up and down my spine. I couldn't tell you how long he threatened to kill me for. It could've been for weeks, maybe a month, but what I do remember is that he reminded me every day. He told me that he knew where I lived and watched me when I was at home. I would go home and shut all of our curtains. My mom thought I didn't like sunlight. Who doesn't like sunlight? The sun is the reason I rise again each day. But as I mentioned before, speaking up for myself has never been my forte.

Even from the age of five, I didn't tell the teachers, I didn't even tell my own mom that I was, what I didn't know at the time, being extremely bullied and harassed. I had a few close girlfriends at the time, and one of them, after witnessing the constant fear I was in, said something to the teachers on my behalf. This boy was confronted and suspended for a week. I remember feeling free that week, letting the wind blow through my hair without looking back to see if he was watching me. I was laughing with my girlfriends on the swings instead of cowering by the teacher on recess duty. But when he came back to school after a week, he came back with a knife. What happened that day was and still is a blur in my memory, but in the end he was expelled.

Reflecting now, I feel really sorry for this young boy, or man now. I wonder to myself, what was going on in his home life? What caused him so much angst towards me? What had happened to him to feel so much anger and want to act upon it? And as for me, I wonder if the reason I never spoke up was because of my empathic nature. That deep down, in my soul, I wanted to help him heal. Even if that was my truth at the time, and I truly believe it was, I can't bypass the fact that this experience was much more traumatic than I ever let it on to be. As the resilient young girl I was, I consciously moved on, learning to not always be looking over my shoulder while enjoying my youth. But subconsciously, this experience taught me that I was never going to be safe, that this fear of losing my life to someone else's hand was inevitable, that this was my fate. As the years went on, I was heavily influenced by the deep-rooted fear that had slithered its way into my soul, like a smoldering black cloud weighing me down, blocking my access to what I know is now my faith crown.

Fear is a heavy feeling. It weighs you down, draining the energy in your body. Fear's job is to make you feel sick and not the kind of sick where you're cooped up in bed, covered up all cozy like a warm cinnamon bun amongst your blankets. No, it's the kind of sickness you feel when you're on a haunted house ride, where ghosts of memories past consume you out of nowhere. Where mummies pop out of coffins in hopes to entangle you so you stay wrapped in the tightly bound clutch of fear. At first, being wrapped in fear felt comforting. Being fearful allowed me to always prepare for the worst. Of course, "the worst" looks different for all of us, but for me, the worst had reared its head many times in my life. Fear was showing up as abandonment, abuse, addiction, bullying, chronic disease, harassment, and rejection. Living in fear mode became my natural state of being. It was like my whole house was on fire. Even when the fire department showed up, a fire would go out in one room only for my whole kitchen to go up in flames in the next. I began to live with these fires burning all around me, smelling smoke, knowing I was trapped and feeling as if there was no way out. That there was never going to be a way out. That there was no way, if you just believe, this so-called "light at the end of the tunnel" would appear, guiding you to the other side, so you can live from a place of faith and not fear.

My fear mindset was fueled by my life experiences. Having been beaten down again and again, I became accustomed to this pain. I let my trauma backpack become so heavy that walking around with it was impossible. And instead of trying to lighten the load, to pick out each memory like a book, to make a promise to myself to not open the book if I didn't have to and dispose of it as needed; I kept it on, sitting down, unable to move by the weight of it. Not moving forward yet still cripplingly anchored in the past. I was refusing to believe that maybe, just maybe, there was an ounce of faith living deep down in my soul. That maybe I could lighten the load, maybe I could release some of the fear that had turned into anxiety, distress, apprehension, and dread. That maybe my thoughts around what fear had represented previously didn't need to stay with me in the present or be carried forth into my future. That perhaps if I began to feed the faith, the fear would start to disappear.

I once heard someone say, "fear is just false evidence appearing real," and this shook me to my itty bitty core. Of course, in my past, I had very real reasons to be fearful, but as I matured, this fear was no longer rational or situational; it was psychological. I was so used to living in this fear mode that I was always preparing for the worst out of fear that something *might* happen. I mentioned that I was a resilient child and that was only depicted as being able to cope with the present moment. As I grew up, I started to let my imagination run wild in fear-land, inevitably not being able to cope with these potential but highly hypothesized situations. When my doctors first found out that my liver was covered in masses (that we now know are tumors), and I began going through what felt like months of endless ultrasounds, CT scans and MRIs; my mind immediately began to prepare for the fact that I might have cancer. We didn't know what the diagnosis was at the time, but the hepatologists, radiologists, surgeons, specialists, were working night and day to figure out what was going on. In my mind, I had to go to the worst-case scenario. This was a result of my habitual worrying from feeding the fear for so long. I was living on the tipping edge of my nerves, and any stressful situation seemed to tip me over. I would fall for what seemed like days, down a rabbit hole, falling victim to the fear over and over again. Until one day, while I was searching for a way to climb out of the rabbit hole, I looked up and saw a small twinkling light. At first, it pierced my eyes, making it difficult to look, and my eyes swelling up with tears every time I tried. But over time, it slowly started to become brighter, lighter, feeling like milk and honey washing over me as I breathed in the energy it radiated, the energy of faith. So that as I continued to inhale, the light of faith grew so large that the rabbit hole was no longer a hole, and I was sitting on the soil of the earth, meditating with the light of faith flooding into my crown chakra as I sipped it up, like my favourite cup of tea.

As I drank in the tea of faith, I felt something I had never felt before — faith in myself. Faith in my ability to heal, to heal my past trauma, to heal my illnesses, to heal my mind, body and soul. In March of 2019, I decided it was time to feed the faith and not the fear. I started to truly believe that I was going to heal from my chronic illnesses, that there was no way I was going to be living a life of what ifs and what could have been because I was afraid of what might come next. I started to believe that the world was truly my oyster and that with all of the roots of my Oak tree, I was ready and supported to live a life from faith. Because, what if what was to come next was…finding ways to balance my hormones so that I wasn't controlled by my chronic pain 24/7. Staying sober for over a year and a half and counting, starting my own business and seeing it thrive, investing in my Yoga Teacher and Yoga Therapy training, investing in my spiritual health and understanding the messages from my intuition led to me becoming an energy healer and writing this book. I could keep going, but the point is I held my faith that all of these things would come true, and they did, they have. It hasn't been easy, and why would I have wanted it to? The best things are never easy, but they are always worth it. Feeding the faith allowed me to work harder at becoming a more active participant in my own healing journey than I had ever before. It also allowed me to see my fears from a new perspective, as opportunities to expand, instead of holding me hostage. So that when my last root began to propagate, pushing its way through the dense soil and into the earth, it flourished through all of the other roots. Almost as if this last root, the root of surrender, was ready to hold them all so they could continue to grow deep down, together; and me my soul, through the branches, growing higher and higher.

13

OM NAMO NAYARANI

(I surrender to the Divine and all its power)

As this next root grew, enveloping all of the space around it, above it, below it, it was filling me with the understanding that it was time to gracefully fall into the abyss of surrendering to the unknown. I wish I could say that this surrender came easy to me, that I let go of the energetic cords of the past as easily as I exhaled. But no, these cords stayed bound tight to my throat for much longer than requested. Like a boa constrictor getting ready to eat its meal, first squeezing the life out of the victim than devouring it whole. The harder I held on, the tighter the chords became. Clinging to the past, holding onto the memories of what could have been, of what I wanted to happen but never happened, seemed much easier to me than surrendering to the unknown of the future. But as Anais Nin says, "And the day came when the risk to remain tight in a bud was more painful than the risk it took to blossom." I knew that I could no longer blossom by staying attached to the events of my past. If I wanted to continue down this path of growth, expansion and overall healing, I had to let go. Because we cannot heal in the same environment that made us sick. And the things, the people, the expectations of myself and others, were all making me sick. This wasn't a sickness like my chronic illnesses, and it wasn't like the pandemic we are currently experiencing. This sickness was my inability to connect with the divine source and surrender to its will. To truly move from living from *my* will to *thy* will so that my crown chakra could remind me that I am spirit and I have access to all of the wisdom within me.

Knowing that I had access to the magical wisdom within me, that I had the innate ability to heal from unbearable chronic pain, sexual trauma, limiting beliefs and a fear mindset, could only happen when I grieved my old life. I had to grieve the past, what had been, the people I lost along the way, the lifestyle I led. Because even though I had and still have no desire to go back to my old life of self-sabotage, it was the way I lived my life for so long. It was a part of me. I had to grieve Maybe, and all of the other demons, because ultimately, those demons tore me down, tossing me down the rabbit hole of my own destruction repeatedly, so I could eventually crawl my way back up and out. Following the guiding light that for so long, I hadn't been able to see because I was used to living in the dark void of my lifetimes past. I had to set my past on fire and let it burn so I could make way for new energy. The new beginnings, like the spring cycle of my healing, were ready to sprout from my branches that had grown so tall, so expansive that they began to act as a shelter to different forms of life.

My sobriety has brought me an infinite amount of blessings, but the most prevalent blessing of all was my ability to reconnect with my spirituality. I have always been a spiritual being, having a strong connection to nature, plants and animals from a young age; being able to read peoples' energies and know when someone has ill intentions. As I used to say when I worked as an Addictions Counsellor, I have a good bullshit detector. Not just when someone is lying to me, but when they are lying to themselves. I was also known as the accountability queen as I always made sure not only the residents but our staff followed through on their commitments. This came from me doing the same. Recovering from an addiction to alcohol that was a crutch for coping with the traumas of my life reminded me that our roots grow deepest where the wind blows strongest. My root of surrender was so encompassing because surrendering to the will of the Divine and all of its power is a lifelong process. The winds around me, this grand Oak tree, will always be blowing, like tests for the soul from the divine source herself, seeing if I choose to micromanage the Universe, or just let go and let be.

Continuing to let go and let be, surrendering to the divine, is a practice. When I started to truly relinquish all control on what was to come next, I reminded myself and still do, that it's a practice. Just like practicing meditation or yoga, some days, it will come naturally, and on others, it will feel forced and uncomfortable. Some days you will breathe the bountiful energetic downloads from spirit so effortlessly, and on others you will be looking for signs or guidance to only have them appear when you were least expecting it. Connecting with my spirituality as a sober adult, which was accompanied by my journey to self-discovery, investing in my soul-self and healing from the inside out, all started with yoga. Yoga will always be my saving grace as my practice has allowed me to become the most aligned and balanced version of myself physically, mentally, emotionally, and, most of all, spiritually. Connecting with my spirituality started to come back to me consciously during yoga classes, like magic seeping into my soul with each inhale and exhale, allowing me to sink deeper into the poses and deeper into my connection with the divine. This then trickled organically into other spiritual practices that I adopted throughout my life.

I have been praying since I can remember. My Grandma Bebe is an actively practicing Christian, and it was very important to her that I follow suit. She taught me the power of prayer before I had any understanding of the power it held. When I was little, I would pray for the health of my family, friends, loved ones, as well as the world. I would pray for the fairy Barbie doll with flying wings. I would pray for my parents to get back together so we could live as a family. As the years went on, I prayed for my dad to stop moving away from me. I prayed for my mom to ease up on her domineering parenting style. I prayed for what I thought were my knights in shining armor to fall in love with me. I prayed for the girls at school to stop inviting the boy to parties who had raped me just to see my reaction. I prayed to be able to do a triple pirouette. I prayed and I prayed and I prayed. But the problem was, I wasn't ready to receive all that I was asking for. My prayers were reasonable, but they weren't things the divine could necessarily give me guidance on in the way that I had expected. I wanted to be visited by an angel and told, "all is well, you're good enough, just as you are, everything you're asking about will go in your favour." If only the signs from the spiritual realm were that obvious. To some, they are. Now in this present moment, I can see the divine energy that governs all of life in the sunrise and sunset, in a full-bodied cloud, in the sparkle of someone's eye when they're speaking about their passions. But when you're first working the prayer muscle that is your connection to spirit, much like reconnecting with your intuition, the messages usually start out small before they can grow tall. I started to truly surrender to the divine when I prayed without being attached to the outcome. Letting the divine source know that I am asking for guidance and I am ready to receive whatever comes my way. Trusting that all will work out as it is supposed to, feeling confident as my connection to my crown chakra had become as essential as breathing. As my prana, my breath, my life force energy pulsated through my body, I knew that I could reconnect with any of my chakras whenever I felt out of alignment. Starting from the root and moving upwards, ending at the crown, so that I could begin to surrender to the will of the divine a little more.

As I write this, I can say, "Om Namo Nayarani" and exhale with the knowing that every particle in my soul, living inside of this thousand-year-old Oak tree, is surrendering. I have come to a point in my life where I wake up before the sun to see it rise, allowing its full-bodied essence to illuminate my entire being.

Filling me with its energy as I wake up, to carry this incandescent feeling with me as I go about my day so that the roots I have worked so hard to keep stable and sturdy can continue to hold me as they have been. I was nourishing my soul-self as the sky fills with hues of pinks, oranges and blues, keeping my vibration high so that no matter what comes my way, I can allow that person or situation to hold its own vibration while I keep tending to mine. Like the branches of my Oak tree, I was beginning to soar to the heavens above, equipped with all of the tools to continue through my cycles of healing. So that when my next winter season of healing came around, I was not only ready but excited to curl up next to the fire that stays ablaze within my soul. The constant I know from this lifetime and past is that the seasons are foreseeable. They come, they go, and then they come again. A constant reminder that if the trees can shed their leaves, so can we. If the trees can accept the life and death cycle, then so can we. And if my soul can become an Oak tree that will live on for thousands of years, breathing new life into me and all other beings, so can yours.

I will leave you with this quote by Lalla, the Kashmiri Saint of Spoken Word,

> "I Lalla, entered through the door of the garden of my mind and saw Shiva and Shakti united into one, O joy!
> There I became immersed in the lake of nectar.
> And died even while I was still alive.
> What can death do to me now?"

As my gift to you, enjoy these meditations, journal prompts and yoga class to assist you as you continue on your healing journey.

https://www.healingwithhannah.ca/divine

Acknowledgments

To my mom, thank you for being my rock. Thank you for supporting me endlessly throughout the many ups and downs that life has thrown my way. Through each and every curve ball you have been by my side, lifting me up, being strong when all I knew was how to be weak. I only hope that one day I can do for you what you have done for me. My love for you flows endlessly. To Popo (my dad), you are one hell of a dad. Thank you for stopping at every play structure that I wanted to play at when I was little. Thank you for allowing the things that mom wouldn't - getting a puppy, Harvey, when I was eleven; and paying for my first tattoo because I was seventeen and underage. You may not have always been there physically but your spirit is something I have cherished since before I was incarnated. To both my parents, I chose you. You gave my physical body life but my spirit chose you two. To be your guides on this ever changing journey of life. I am here to help you heal and I hope that after reading my book, you know, you both have helped me heal, every step of the way.

To my best friend and soulmate, Josh, thank you for continuously showing me how much you love and appreciate me. You are the man of my dreams, the yang to my yin, you keep grounded while I tend to float away. You have driven miles across Canada for me, jumping in head first to a long-distance relationship that neither of us thought would turn into a life partnership. But I know we both wouldn't have it any other way. I am looking forward to continuing to build a life with you and starting this next chapter together.

To my step-dad, thank you for taking me as your own even when I pulled away. You have shown me unwavering kindness, support and a little tough love along the way.

To my step-mom, or should I say, step-monster, Lisa, you have been in my life for as long as I can remember. You were there when I got my first period and showed me how to use a pad. You drove me to almost every dance class and there were A LOT of dance classes over the years. You showed me how to use make-up but also how to love myself for the badass Wonder Woman that I am. Thank you for being my biggest cheerleader, I am forever grateful for the way you have helped shape me into me.

To Sandra, thank you for your calm, warm and inviting energy. You are a gift to this world and my dad is lucky to have you in his life.

To all of my soul sisters, you know who you are, thank you

for always being down for my shenanigans. For supporting me when I was at my worst and inspiring me when I am at my best. For buying me groceries, bringing me fries, sending me flowers and just being the intergalactic, cosmic beings that you are.

Thank you to my best friend, Kim, you helped me get through my dark days of winter in Toronto. Thank you for letting me basically live with you throughout our Undergrads. Thank you for always being my model, my muse. Thank you for getting last minute tattoos with me on my last day in Toronto before moving home. I am forever in love with you and our friendship.

Thank you to Ashley-Ann, my amazing book coach, you have believed in me throughout this process more than I believed in myself. Your endless reminders of how powerful my story is, kept me going during times where I felt like giving up. You are innately talented, you have a gift and I am privileged to have been able to work with you.

To my peer reviewers, Margarita & Nick, my fellow artists, thank you for being the mystical beings that you are and taking the raw version of my book into your hands and taking such sweet care. Your magic is woven throughout and your comments allowed my wisdom to flow more effortlessly. You both inspire me to be a better version of me, everyday.

Thank you to my business coach and long lost sister, Danielle.

ENTERING THE DIVINE, ONE BREATH AT A TIME

You are a woman of true beauty and grace. You have changed my life in more ways than I can count. Your compassionate nature is one of a kind and I have been blessed to have had you as a past boss, current coach but most of all, friend.

To my therapist, Anne, I don't have enough thank you's to say or give to you. You have held space for me in ways that I have never experienced. I have worked through lifetimes of trauma because of your guidance and assistance. I know you will continue to change lives, as you already are.

Thank you to my book designer, Dave and my editor, Devlyn, both of you put your heart and soul into helping me birth my book. I wouldn't be here without you two and I thank you for all of the hard-work, time and dedication you put into helping my story come to life.

To Nicole, thank you for creating the most beautiful music for my audio meditations that are included on the bonus landing page that accompanies *Entering the Divine, One Breath at a Time*.

Thank you to **you**, the reader. For picking up my book. For diving head first into my story, a story that gently swallows you whole so when you emerge, you start to recognise your own healing and growth. And I hope that you have recognized this. That you are growing and healing and that my story has just been a loving witness to your own divine development.

About the Author

Hannah Stinson was born on November 13, 1992 and raised in Winnipeg, Canada. From a young age Hannah has had a strong connection to her spirituality and was considered an old soul by elders in her life. Hannah has experienced lifetimes of hardship in her short time on Earth but it has never dampened her spirit. She is a woman of true resilience and pure strength. Hannah was diagnosed with endometriosis at the age of 23 and liver disease at the age of 26, both of which have had a serious impact on her physical health but allowed her to flourish in other aspects of her healing journey. Hannah is an advocate for yoga as she has been practicing for over a decade and is currently completing her 200 hour Yoga Teacher Training (YTT200) and will be done at the end of 2020. Once she has completed her YTT200 she dives right into her 400 hour Yoga Therapy certification. Practicing yoga has changed Hannah's life, she has learned that the teachings we learn on our mat can be applied in everyday life, the more comfortable you can be in an uncomfortable posture, the more comfort you can find in uncomfortable situations in life. At the end of the day, all we have to do is breathe through it.

She graduated from Ryerson University's School of Fashion with a Bachelor of Design which was the catalyst for her path to becoming a Feminine Healing Coach. During her final year, she had to complete an undergraduate capstone project and she chose to bring awareness and educate about endometriosis through art and technology. Her art exhibit, Love Thy Lady Parts, was the first time she felt empowered again. During her panel evaluation, where there were 4 judges determining her final grade, she was granted an A+, and every single judge told her that she was meant to help others heal through creativity and compassion. From there Hannah went on to volunteer at the Indefinite Arts Centre in Calgary, Alberta, teaching art to those with physical and mental disabilities. This heartfelt work reminded her how much she loved to be a part of people's healing journey's. In 2018 she started working as an addiction's counsellor, in the all women's program, Breezy Point at the Behavioural Health Foundation (BHF). During her two years of working there, she started an art program, integrated weekly meditation and yoga classes, facilitated community sessions helping to enhance boundaries, positive self-talk, self-care activities and self-worth, to name a few. She also secured a $5,000 Art Grant through the Jewish Women's Endowment Fund, which allowed her to build the art program she created so that the women could continue to grow and flourish as artists. Throughout the two years that Hannah worked at BHF, she obtained over 10 different certifications, some of which include, Life Coaching (Spiritual & Therapeutic Art), PTSD & Addictions Counseling, and Non-Violent Crisis Intervention.

HANNAH STINSON

Hannah has always been extremely ambitious, she started working at the age of 15 and has had over 30 different jobs, working in the following industries, administration, arts & culture, counselling, customer service, digital media, entertainment, event organization, fashion, holistic health, marketing, mental health, and sales, to name a few. Throughout her career, she has learned the common theme that brings her joy is helping others become active participants in their own healing journey's and that is why she started *Healing with Hannah*. *Healing with Hannah* was a business born throughout the Covid19 pandemic. Hannah had to make the hard decision, along with the testament of her doctors, to not work at BHF any longer due to being the immune compromised and working in a high risk environment. This broke her heart but was also a blessing in disguise, as it opened her eyes to the realization that she was meant to be an entrepreneur. Becoming a Feminine Healing Coach has been a dream come true for Hannah. She is able to work one-on-one, as well as in group settings with womxn who are willing and ready to be active participants in their own healing journey's. Hannah incorporates practices such as, but not limited to, embodiment, emotional freedom technique (EFT or tapping), meditation, neuro linguistic programming, somatic resourcing, tarot card reading and yoga, throughout her programs, sessions and offers. To work with Hannah or find out more about *Healing with Hannah*, head to www.healingwithhannah.ca.

Manufactured by Amazon.ca
Acheson, AB

13419209R00069